Dear Gale,

Thank you for your support.
Keep making a difference.

David Farmer
Smith

STRAIGHTEN UP

AND

FLY RIGHT

UNLOCKING YOUR FULL POTENTIAL

by

David Larrick Smith

Inspirational Speaker, Author, and Consultant

authorHOUSE®

AuthorHouse™
1663 Liberty Drive, Suite 200
Bloomington, IN 47403
www.authorhouse.com
Phone: 1-800-839-8640

First published by AuthorHouse 3/31/2009

ISBN: 978-1-4343-7228-4 (sc)

Printed in the United States of America
Bloomington, Indiana

This book is printed on acid-free paper.

TABLE OF CONTENTS

Acknowledgments

To my Maker

I acknowledge and thank you, dear God, for my ability and passion. I thank you for all that I am...for my many blessings and the vision you have bestowed upon me...for the discipline to complete this work and to do your will—Amen.

To my Family and Friends

I am the man I am today because of the effort of so many people. I am the fruit of their labor. God bless my parents, David G. Smith Jr. and Alyce Pearl Smith. Their struggle for basic human dignity and civil rights was fought so that I could experience the freedom and opportunity that facilitated this work, and the wonderful quality of life I now enjoy. I am forever in their debt.

I have friends who let me get on my soapbox and shout, debate, and many times talk over them. God bless you all for your patience and acceptance of me and my idiosyncrasies. I love you all: Patrick and Christina Coker, Dale Klied, Eric Williamson, Brian and Denise Parker, Michael and Charonda Hermens, and Ryan "The Marlboro Man" Hayes

To my Supporters

Thank you for supporting me with the purchase of this book. To your success and happiness!

To my Glorious Wife

> "I will love you 'til your hair turns gray, yeah…,
> And I'll still want you if you gain a little weight, girl…,
> The way I feel for you will always be the same,
> just as long as your love don't change."
> *- Musiq Soulchild*

I love my wife like the movies! At least one of those great romantic love stories that always pulls on your heartstrings, and the characters' dreams come true! Words are truly too weak to define the depth of love and the level of commitment I have for my wonderful wife. She is regal, elegant, and sophisticated, while being warm, compassionate, and approachable. Thank you for keeping me on track and keeping me grounded. She is the reigning Ms. Caribbean of New York! ***All Hail My Queen!***

PREFACE

Millions of people get stuck in the quagmire of mediocrity. Most people buy into the average. They allow the world to make choices for them, and they become apathetic through the process. They buy into the concept that they have no control over their lives, and by relinquishing control to chance, they become nay-sayers who turn opportunities into obstacles and possibilities into problems. These people do not understand the Natural Laws that govern human potential, and if they do, they choose to ignore them and live in ignorance of them. Failure, then, is a choice.

You probably know someone who is stuck in life and has lost all hope of ever doing anything great or attaining real holistic success[1]. Unfortunately, many people simply don't believe that success is possible for them, and that is the ultimate problem. Bible scripture teaches us: "As a man thinketh in his heart, so is he!" Proverbs 23:7.

You may even be one of "those" people. I was! I allowed my previous programming and lack of self-discipline to keep me stuck. If you live with pain long enough, you will find a way to rationalize, accept, and exist in that pain. That's exactly what I did for years! I actually knew what I could do to improve my life, but I played the victim and felt entitled to be mad at God and the world for all my unhappiness. There were/are opportunities in abundance all around me (and you too), but my anger clouded my vision and logic. My issue was that I simply chose to believe in, and work with, the wrong information. I had to forgive myself for the mistakes of the past thirty-plus years. I had to suck it up, dust myself off, and move on with new information that was proven to get the right results, and is also irrefutable!

---

[1] Real Holistic Success—A desired balance of physical well being, loving relationships, worthy goals, inner peace, and financial freedom.

We are all born geniuses, yet most of us take our talents to the grave—the statistics show that. Once I got sick and tired of being sick and tired, I chose to do more with my life. I began working on myself. I took responsibility for my happiness. I forgave myself for making mistakes, living in ignorance, and making poor decisions. I stopped focusing on what I was afraid of, and began focusing on what I wanted in my life. I created positive expectations for myself. I changed my thinking, and therefore changed my actions. When I changed my actions, my results changed too. So YOU must do the same! To change your reality you must change your thinking! You must strive for excellence daily, and constantly work on your own personal development. You must create habit patterns that produce successful results, habits that will lead you toward your goals and toward manifesting your potential. You are who you are today because of your efforts from the past. The person you will become tomorrow depends on the efforts you make today! This book will help you do that.

This book draws from the summation of thousands of hours and hundreds of years of research by some of the best personal development experts in the world, experts who have studied human behavior and formulated some of the content and methodologies contained in this work. Personal development professionals, psychologists, entrepreneurs, social scientists, theologians, and philanthropists have spent decades and millions of dollars studying human potential and achievement—time and money you don't have to waste! When properly applied, this information is guaranteed to transform your life for the better. *Straighten Up and Fly Right* is a reference book that you should use, read, and re-read to get the best from yourself. You should refer to it often. It contains action items designed to help you maximize your day-to-day performance in every aspect of your life.

I believe that God put us all here to do great things! I believe that if you choose to, that you can accomplish anything you desire! When you believe and have faith, you don't have to hope. When you believe and have faith, you develop peace and comfort because you **know** that the result you want is going to happen. I believe that I can achieve anything that my mind can conceive! I also believe that when I master myself, and my God-given talents, I will change the world for the betterment of mankind! This book is one of the many steps necessary to making that goal a reality. By helping others to manifest their talents and contribute their greatness to our society, I will impact the world in the way that God intended. I know this information can help you if you put it to work in your life.

This work is broken into three sections: My Story, The Problem, and The Solution. My story gives you a snapshot of my life: who I am, where I'm from, what I believed, and where I went wrong. Part Two focuses on problem identification, because knowing is truly half the battle. I focus on some of the major factors that hinder most people in the pursuit of unlocking their potential, achieving their goals, and attaining real holistic success. Finally, Part Three broaches solutions that helped me turn my life around; it focuses on the information and tactics that will transform your life and put you on the path to having all that you desire.

"Trust in the LORD with all your heart and lean not on your own understanding; in all your ways acknowledge Him, and He will make your paths straight."

Proverbs 3:5-6

INTRODUCTION

November 5, 2007. I was actually just about done with this body of work when I read the following paragraph from the book *Until Today* and felt compelled to include it:

> *The greatest service I can offer is a clear and loving message. People do not have to hear your message. When you are given a message, an insight, a revelation, your only responsibility is to deliver what you have been given. What happens once the message is delivered is not, is NOT, your responsibility. If you judge the correctness, accuracy or power of your message based on how it is received, you will miss the point. Once you, the messenger, miss the point, the message is lost.*
>
> Iyanla Vanzant, Author

I frequently do a poor job of following my own advice, and my interpretation of my experience in the world can sometimes be that people are cynical, apathetic, and cold. Ms. Vanzant's point hit me so hard, because I sometimes feel like I am not making a difference, that people/society does not hear my message and maybe I should not say it. Maybe I should not care as much as I do. I begin to despair. But I aspire to grow every day by studying, reading, and spiritualizing with books like Ms. Vanzant's—I always find tidbits of inspiration that keep me going...so I do. I know that my job is merely to give the message; it's your job to choose to hear it. Enjoy!

Have you ever tried removing a screw with the wrong type of screwdriver? The task can be done, but it is very frustrating. You may work very hard and diligently at removing the screw, but the harder you work, the more damage you do to the head of the screw, and if you strip the head of the screw, it will require even more tools and resources to remove it. You could possibly fall behind on other tasks trying to remove the screw, and even damage the project you are working on.

So many people go through life damaging themselves because they are using the wrong tools and information for goal attainment, or they are ignorant of the tools and information altogether. So they work even harder in the wrong job, career, or industry getting the wrong results, with the wrong people, in the wrong occupation—all the while, creating more and more stress, frustration, heartache in their lives and dysfunctionality in their family. Are you getting what you want out of life? Are you really happy with the direction your life is headed?

When we have experiences, we always tell others about them. A typical example would be the last restaurant, or a movie you've patronized. Good or bad, you usually tell someone. If the experience impacts you in a significant way, you'll become even more animated when describing the effects to others. Such is the case with the information in this book. By using the information and tactics contained in this book, I have been able to: discover my passion and life's work, create my own successful business, achieve financial congruence, marry the woman of my dreams, build a dream home, travel the world, and find the freedom and peace of mind that I have always prayed for. I want you to experience the balanced success that I have found. I want to tell you about what I've done, and how I've done it. If you want to achieve similar results in your life, and experience a higher level of fulfillment and happiness, then you're reading one of the right books. You have taken a major step towards developing yourself and manifesting your potential!

I chose to write this book for many reasons, and all of them encompass my family, friends, and extended support groups. I want to be of service to those around me. I want to leave a legacy of contribution and to impact my community, nation, and planet in a way that God intended. However, when I discovered the following statistics I developed a new sense of urgency regarding spreading this information. I want you to remember these statistics as you read this book. This information is completely unnerving to me, and should be to you, because it is FACTUAL! This is not my opinion. This is not speculation. This is happening to people in America as you read this—and not just a few people, but most people.

The US Department of Health and Human Services reports that by the age of 65, for every 100 people in America, the following statistics hold true:

- 29 will be dead
- 13 will live below the poverty level
- 54 will be dependent on charity, welfare, or social security
- 4 will be financially free

Only 4 people out of every 100 attain financial freedom! I was absolutely floored. I also internalized an ugly reality: this was happening to me, and I was heading down this road! It was happening to my family, and it was happening to everyone around me. I couldn't think of anyone in my immediate, or extended, support group who had achieved financial freedom or real holistic success. Money is not the most important thing in life, but it is like water and air: you have to have it to survive in this world, but it is not everything.

How can this be the result of so many decades of work and effort? I can understand this happening to people who don't work or loaf around all their lives trying to scam the system looking for a hand-out and not applying themselves, but these statistics represent the hardest working members of American society. These are hard-working folks, people who have worked very hard for thirty to forty years contributing to society and making an effort. This is America—the richest country in the world! We live in a time of immense affluence, limitless opportunity, and gross wealth. How could so many people end up like this? The statistics don't lie. These are cold, hard numbers.

In 1989 I began studying personal development and self-help information in an effort to improve my life, but it wasn't until 2001 that I actually began to internalize and apply the priceless information. This meant that for twelve years, my limited belief system invalidated all the new self-help personal development information. As a child I was told by my mother that I had tremendous potential, and that I could do anything that I set my mind to do. I believed what my momma said. I believed that I would do great things with my life. So in 2001, on the verge of a nervous breakdown because I was miserable, over-worked, over-stressed, overweight, in a job that I hated with no future of advancement and no significance, existing from check to check, and saddled with thousands of dollars in consumer debt…I wondered: **"Where did I go wrong?"** I thought to myself: "I'm a good person of Christian faith, I've worked extremely hard, I've been disciplined, I've been of service to others, and I've earned my college degree—I've done my best." I felt like I had done what society had asked of me. Where was my American dream?

My momma raised me to work hard and to always do my best. She would say: "Just do your best honey, that's all you can do!" I believed that "doing my best" would be enough. But my efforts had not led me to balance, peace of mind, happiness, or financial freedom. So what do you think I did about my situation? I worked even harder! Working harder must be the answer…right? Wrong! Even though most Americans work extremely hard and diligently for forty-plus years, most people have to go back to work in their golden years just to exist; in the never-ending pursuit of the all mighty dollar, we neglect the emotional, physical, and spiritual areas of our lives even more.

WHY? Why does this happen? More importantly: how do you avoid being one of the 96 out of 100 who don't make it and who end up broke, alone, unfulfilled, sickly, and dependent on someone else for their existence? The answer to both of these questions and many others concerning the realization of your full potential and real holistic success are contained in this book. Sound too good to be true? Well, just keep reading. Before 2001, I had basically bought into the wrong information regarding goal attainment and high achievement. My old beliefs were based on information that simply didn't lead me towards the results that I wanted; therefore, regardless of how good my intentions were, or how noble my efforts, or how hard I worked, I was using the wrong information—so I got the wrong results. This concept is at the core of why so many people never achieve real holistic success. Most people never figure out or internalize the very simple concept of working smarter vs. working harder.

What if you don't have to make the mistakes I made? What if you knew the success secrets (or should I say success information, because the information is not a secret) of the greatest and most successful minds of the last two thousand years? What if you could shorten the learning curve to attaining real holistic success? What if you could learn to win while eliminating common mistakes and developing skills that would put you on the path to success, significance, and self-actualization [2]? How would you use that information? Well that's exactly what you're holding right now! I wrote this book for the sole purpose of helping you to internalize the correct information for manifesting your potential, to share and teach the information that leads to real holistic success. If someone in my life had shared this information with me at age thirteen, I believe that I would have manifested all that potential my momma spoke of ten to fifteen years ago. Even so, I'm still one of the lucky ones, in that I have discovered my passion in life at a relatively young age; most people never do. Now I must begin a new process, and plant new seeds. I must complete the work of manifesting my passion, and by doing so, I believe that I will help others to do the same. YOU must do the same!

Helpful Definitions

I discovered my passion by simply using the good sense God gave me. If it makes good sense, then use it! One of the most fundamental keys to success is to model successful people. Do what successful people do, the way successful people do them, and you can experience what successful people experience. So does this make good sense so far? That said, there are some concepts and

---

[2] Self-actualization—The intrinsic growth of what is already in the organism, or more accurately, of what the organism is. (*Psychological Review*, 1949)

definitions I want to introduce, as I will refer to them often throughout this book.

DEFINING SUCCESS

For the sake of clarity, let me explain what I think success is. The way I define success may not mean success to you. Success is like love. No one can tell you what love is. You must define love for yourself. Defining success works the same way. Success is a state of mind that is purely subjective in our existence, and must be defined by each of us. In his tape series *Lead the Field*, Earl Nightingale defines success as "the progressive realization of a worthy goal." He also states that human beings are happiest during the pursuit of their goals, rather than in the actual achievement of them. He explains that the process and experiences along the way to achieving our goals are what we enjoy and remember most.

Example:
Think about the holiday season. During those few weeks leading up to Christmas, we experience a tremendous sense of anticipation and excitement as we eagerly count down the arrival of Christmas. Most people are friendlier and more generous those days leading up to Christmas. We participate in holiday traditions like decorating Christmas trees, our homes, and our communities. We buy and wrap gifts for loved ones. We share and we care! Our homes tend to smell of fresh baked goods, and we eat and enjoy foods that we only see or experience during the holidays. There is a whole series of events that exemplify the holiday season. However, on Christmas Day, there is a sort of letdown. A finality begins to fill the air because Christmas is now here, the goal successfully achieved. Christmas Day is actually the end of the journey. It was the ramping up that started the day after Thanksgiving, and went right up to 11:59pm on December 24th, that created the most excitement! It was the days between Thanksgiving and Christmas that were the most enjoyable. It was the "progressive realization" that gave us the most pleasure and enjoyment. Even though I cannot define success for you, I think

there are several common denominators that people look for when describing real holistic success. Many qualities will come to mind, but I believe that there are five major areas in life that all definitions and/or qualities of real holistic success will fall into. So as you read this book, when I mention real holistic success, I want you to think about the following characteristics.

PHYSICAL WELL-BEING

I think the most important thing in life is your health and strength. Without it you are dead, literally! What good is all the money in the world, if you are too sick to spend and enjoy what it can provide? What if you have a great family and loving relationships, but you can't visit your loved ones' home for a barbecue because you are bedridden due to physical illness? American society is so occupied with making money that we neglect one of the most important facets of our lives: our health.

PURPOSE / GOALS

Every person on this planet has been put here to do something specific and something great. We are not designed for mediocrity; that we learn from our environment and through poor choices in life. You can only find true happiness doing what you love to do.

INNER PEACE

Every year at Christmas my wife asks me what I want for Christmas, and every year I tell her: "peace of mind." With all the things in my life (running a business, personal commitments, family issues, retirement planning, healthcare, civic responsibilities, volunteerism, and the miscellaneous activities) I just want to know that I am doing what God put me here to do, and that I am getting that work done. Peace of mind is the ability to be totally at peace with yourself, your finances, your family, your community, your station in life, and the direction in which your life is heading. Most people that I have surveyed list "being comfortable or at peace" as a major goal in their lives. You will never attain real holistic success without inner peace.

PRODUCTIVE RELATIONSHIPS

Someone once said: "all the money in the world is worthless unless you have someone to share it with." An independent survey conducted on the D.A.R.T. (Dallas Area Rapid Transit) Light Rail system confirmed 95% of respondents said the first thing they would do if they won the lottery was to help their friends and families.

FINANCIAL CONGRUENCE

Is money important? Of course it is. Pursuing large sums of money, with the philosophy that money will solve your problems is simply a train wreck in the making. Research has shown that a huge percentage of millionaire lottery winners eventually squander the money and end up in the same financial state they were in before they won the lottery. In the book *Secrets of the Millionaire Mind*, author T. Harv Eker explains: "The vast majority of people simply do not have the internal capacity to create and hold on to large amounts of money and the increased challenges that go with more money and success." This is a major point to embrace. Truly successful people develop a mindset of abundance and growth, where most people just strive to "get by" and hold on to the present.

What is financial congruence? I think it is having enough money so that you don't worry about the things money provides, or the things the lack of money keeps you from having. Basically, having enough money to provide the quality of life you desire for the rest of your life. This is also a subjective point. For some people a hundred thousand dollars a year is the magic number; for others a million dollars wouldn't be enough. You have to determine how much you need and what amount will do it for you.

The objective of *Straighten Up and Fly Right* is to help you attain a modicum of success in each of the aforementioned areas—to help you create balance in you life! To help you transform your thinking. As you continue reading, I think having a clear understanding of what I mean regarding success is tremendously important; concurrently, understanding the following principles is also paramount.

NATURAL LAW AND META-PHYSICAL PRINCIPLES

Have you ever gotten a ticket from a police officer for doing something you did not know was illegal? Imagine the following scenario.

Example:
Officer: "License and registration please."
You: "Is there a problem, officer?"
Officer: "You made an illegal right turn at the intersection."
You: "I didn't know that I couldn't turn right on red at this intersection…"
Officer: "It's your responsibility to know the rules of the road."

Then you receive your moving violation.

Moral of the story: ignorance of the law is not an excuse from the consequences of breaking it.

There are several principles and concepts that I want you to understand as they are the keys to high performance and success. I will frequently refer to them throughout this book. These laws affect human beings, our planet, and everything on it equally. These laws have also been referred to as Universal Laws or Natural Principles. Efficacy of these laws has nothing to do with your race, gender, education, nationality, geography, socioeconomic background, pedigree, or sexual orientation. Each of us is equally affected by natural law. We can consciously use them to our benefit, or live in ignorance of them to our detriment. The overwhelming statistics show that most people do the latter.

The Law of Belief—Whatever you choose to believe becomes your reality. An additional caveat of the Law of Belief is that your beliefs also form a filter for new information. Anything that conflicts with what you have chosen to believe, your mind will filter out.

The Law of Return—We reap what we sow. You cannot reap until you first sow.

The Law of Causality—For every effect in the world, there is a cause. There is a reason for everything. Your thoughts are the causes, and your circumstances are the effects.

The Law of Expectation—You will live a life consistent with what you expect. The universe will provide you with exactly what you ask for and expect.

The Principle of Manifestation—Your thoughts determine your feelings. Your feelings determine your actions. Your actions determine your results.

The Principle of Conservation of Momentum—The total amount of momentum of all the things in the universe will never change. One of the consequences of this is that the center of mass of any system of objects will always continue with the same velocity unless acted on by a force outside the system. If you don't like the direction your life is headed, you must take affirmative action to change your direction.

The Winning Edge Principle—Small differences in your effort can equate to huge differences in your results.

Degree Theory™—A popular school of thought that believes: if you want to be successful in life (basically as I defined it) you need to go to school and earn a college degree.

"Nothing in the world is more dangerous than sincere ignorance and conscientious stupidity."

Reverend Dr. Martin Luther King, Jr.

Part One

My Story

Chapter One

In The Beginning

Sincere ignorance and conscientious stupidity—that was a great way to sum up my life. Are your efforts going to make you 1 of the 4 out of every 100 people who make it, or 1 of the 96 that don't? Well, during the first twenty-five years of my life, I was headed for the 96 percentile. This is my story.

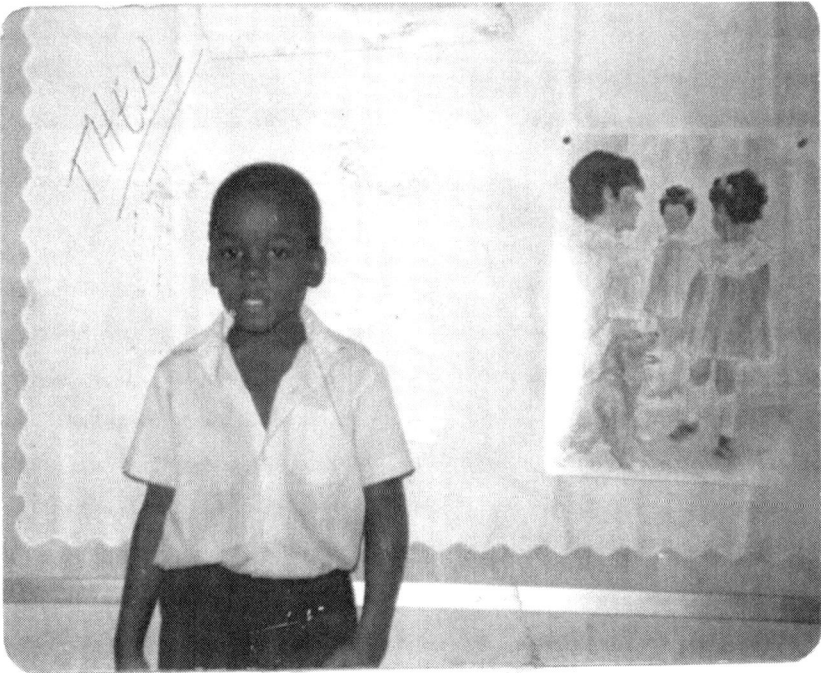

I will give you the abridged version of my story as this is not an autobiography, but I think it is worth mentioning because I think I'm a pretty average guy. I was born into a working class African-American family in Garland, Texas, a small city east of Dallas. I am the middle child of three. I have an older brother, who was my childhood idol and hero, and a younger sister whom I adore. Each of us were born four years apart. As a child, right up until high school, I was a short, plump, and not very coordinated; basically, I was a short, fat kid. I dealt with all the persecution that went along with being short, fat, unpopular, and relatively poor. I didn't have any of the name-brand accoutrements of adolescence in the '80s: the Jordache designer jeans, parachute pants, polo shirts, leather Dr. Jay's, or a Members Only jacket—all of which you needed for social validation and acceptance. Contrary to my situation, my brother was in the "in-crowd." He was able to acquire some of the material things and was very athletic, good looking, and popular. This compounded my situation as an individual, as I lost my identity. I wasn't David, I was Tony's little brother; but I was cool with that because I looked up to him—I wanted to be like him. Not so much because of his popularity, but because he seemed to be validated and accepted by his peers and other people. I was a misfit.

My parents were blue-collar municipal employees. My father worked for the City of Garland at the city warehouse, and my momma worked as a nurse at Garland Memorial Hospital. As Dick Gregory once wrote: "We ain't poor, we just broke!" We didn't have much. Looking back, I now realize that my family had it pretty good compared to a lot of folks in our neighborhood: I had both parents in my life, they had jobs, and we seemed to have stability—relatively speaking. My environment was a curious paradox. On one hand it was very nurturing—like the African proverb: "the village raised the children." Other times it was downright violent! We all lived on the "eastside." I find it interesting that most cities in America have an "eastside," and the inhabitants on that side always seem to struggle.

My maternal grandmother lived on Parker Circle, and we lived around the corner not to far from her on Richard St., right across the street from Cooter's convenience store at the intersection of Dairy Road and State Highway 66. Parker Circle was adjacent to the infamous Rainbow Apartments, the scariest place to live in Garland at that time. Isn't it ironic that the ugliest, harshest, meanest environments seem to have some of the prettiest, most colorful names? I heard stories that even the police were afraid to go into the Rainbow Apartments. I don't know if that story was true, but I never saw the police in there. There was no pot of gold at the end of that Rainbow. I can make jokes now, but that place was treacherous!

I saw and experienced things that no person, especially a child, should ever have to see: gang violence, alcoholism, poverty, drug abuse, and emotional abuse—all before the age of ten. As my childhood slipped away, I watched schoolmates and relatives get into trouble with the law and eventually end up in county jail, the state penitentiary, or worse: dead. I actually saw a man shot and bleed to death right in front of my grandparents' house on Southwood Drive. I remember hearing the statistics on my chances in life: 1 in 4 African-American males between the ages of seventeen to twenty-five would be hooked on drugs, incarcerated, or dead.

Around the age of nine or ten years old, in the middle of all this chaos, I thought to myself: "How do I improve my situation? How do I either make my neighborhood a better place to live, or get out and make a better home somewhere else?" I didn't personally know anyone who was making it. We all lived on the "eastside." All I ever saw around me was more of the same: poverty, violence, limited thinking, abuse, desperation, drugs, and alcohol. All these realities brought about constant and predictable events. Random acts of violence weren't so random. I don't mention any of this to sensationalize the harsh nature of my childhood—everything was not always doom and gloom—but it was a very rough environment. I'm also not trying to impress you or build street credibility; I am simply trying to impress upon you that even in the ugliest circumstances, life, and the life you make, is STILL about choices. I chose to find a better way to live.

Krystalon, Tony, and David Larrick - 1979

I spent a lot of time dreaming about what life would be like living in a place where all these ugly things were not an everyday occurrence. Deep down I knew there was a better way to live; I just didn't know how to make it happen. There were kids at school who had nice things. Sometimes, when I took the long way home, I would pass by their houses and see what I perceived to be wealth. On Halloween, my cousins and I would go trick or treating in their neighborhood. We called it the "rich folks' houses." The homes were so big and elaborate. They would also be completely brand new homes or relatively new, which was foreign to me. A new house for my family was a different pre-existing home on another street in the same hood! I use to dream of having more, doing more, and being more. My momma and some of the elders in our community like Ms. Madea Hubbard or Mr. C. (Charles Stimpson) would always say things like: "Lark...ya' can do anythang ya' set cha mind ta do!" Miss Essie (Mr. C's wife) would say to me: "Lark...ya gotta press-a-veer!" My middle name is Larrick, but everyone called me Lark or Davalark (pronounced Day-va-lark). This is the South, ya' know—everyone has a nickname. This was also a time when the whole village raised the children. These adults had just as much influence on me as my parents did. But I always pondered their advice: "If setting your mind to achieve a goal and hard work are all it takes to become successful, then why aren't more people around me setting their mind to do better?" I couldn't understand why my family and our community struggled so much when everyone was working so hard. It didn't seem to be a lack of effort that kept everyone back. I didn't understand how so many people could work so hard and still not get ahead.

Dallas Zoo 1979
My Pop's was "Da Man" in those slacks!

As I asked questions about success, there were two answers that always came back, and they were the same everywhere I went. The first thing a person needed to do in order to become successful and live a better life was to work hard. Ok, been there done that—I got that one. The other thing was something that no one in my immediate family or environment had acquired. There was one thing that would allow me to improve my circumstances, make real money, and have success. It would give me a chance to call the shots. I would be able improve my social standing, eat better food, have better clothes, and live in a nice house. I wouldn't have to do physical/manual labor and work in the Texas heat anymore. I would be able to help my family and maybe retire my mother. I would be able to change the financial future of my family and positively affect my community. Everyone I talked to said the same thing: in order to make your dreams a reality, you need to get a college degree.

MY BELIEFS

From as far back as I can remember, Degree Theory™ was extolled as the key for unlocking the door of success in life. Degree Theory™ is a concept I coined to describe the following school of thought: if a person wants to become successful in life, that person needs to go to school and earn a college degree. The individual with a college degree will be better prepared for life and have more opportunities than the person who does not have a college degree.

I was told by everyone around me that if I wanted to be successful, going to college and earning a degree was the way to make it happen. But how was I going to do that? I couldn't afford it. I was not a great student. I didn't even know which school I should go to, or what to major in; but I BELIEVED what they said! I BELIEVED that once attained, a college degree would open the doors of opportunity for me and the success I dreamed about would be possible. That notion, that theory, became my plan to attain success. I staked my whole life on it. I focused all my energy and effort on getting a college degree. Hard work and Degree Theory™ were the keys to changing my life, my family, and my entire existence for the better. I began immediately. (More on Degree Theory™ in chapter four.)

"Think not of yourself as the architect of your career but as the sculptor. Expect to have to do a lot of hard hammering and chiseling and scraping and polishing."

B. C. Forbes,
Founder, *Forbes Magazine*

My Work Ethic

My parents frequently said: "Money doesn't grow on trees!" They instilled the values of work ethic, pride, self-reliance, fairness, and the fear of God in all of us. My momma instilled the fear of Alyce Pearl too! My momma is a "true school" momma! She is the cutest little lady at 4 feet 11.99999 inches tall and pudgy. But don't be fooled by her size. She says what she means, and means what she says. Unlike contemporary parents, she doesn't repeat herself. She is like E. F. Hutton: when she speaks, we listen. She doesn't tolerate disrespect from us in any form. She is a strict disciplinarian. She is fair, honest, and she expects the absolute best from all of us. By the way, this old school home training is what kids lack today. Kids are not different from kids of yesterday; the parents are different. Parents make excuses for their kids and don't expect excellence from kids today. Home training is not taught anymore.

A wonderful by-product of work ethic is a deep sense of appreciation—a lesson parents of today need to internalize and teach their kids. Contemporary parents have created the entitlement generation by not instilling work ethic and the lesson of earning like my parents taught me. It's really not completely our kids' fault that they are so lazy and unappreciative. Most kids today have never had to work or earn anything. I see parents making excuses for their kids. Parents make statements like: "I want to give my kids the things I didn't have growing up." The problem with that philosophy is that a sense of entitlement vs. a sense of responsibility is created. I think parents should give their children the opportunity to earn all the things they didn't have when they were growing up. If parents today did that, the issue of unappreciative kids would not be so pervasive. I know that I'll get criticized for this position, but there's a saying: "the truth will set you free!"

Because of these principles, I was willing to do whatever I could to earn a buck, as long as it was legal. I was six or seven years old when I began my first entrepreneurial endeavor: I sold pressed ham sandwiches and Kool-Aid® to the kids playing basketball at Ms. Madea's house across the street. I didn't wait for something to happen—I made something happen:

- I swept the floor at Stark's Barbershop
- I walked the neighborhood with my grandmother looking for aluminum cans and bottles to recycle
- I raked leaves and cut grass
- I hung door hangers and grocery store circulars
- I broke down boxes and took out the trash at the Minyard's grocery store
- I even refurbished toys and clothes from the Disabled American Veterans (D.A.V.) trash can. *One man's trash is another man's treasure.*

DANIEL HUMPHRIES/Special to the Daily News
**David Smith of South Garland gets these two the easy
way in Friday's bi-district contest against Spruce.**

WILLIAM E. LAMB/Daily News
South Garland basketball coach Garland Nichols gives up his chair for senior David Smith to sign with Western Texas College in Snyder, Texas. Nichols said in two years with coach Tony Mauldin, Smith could be one of the most recruited junior college players in the state.

"Should you find yourself in a chronically leaking boat, energy devoted to changing vessels is likely to be more productive than energy devoted to patching leaks."

Warren Buffet, Investor

CHAPTER TWO

THE FALLACY

Those miscellaneous jobs taught me that hopes and dreams are worthless without intelligent, focused, diligent work. Today, I am frequently criticized for having expectations that most people consider too high. I hear statements like: "Everybody doesn't think like you, Dave, your expectations are unrealistic!" Well, these people are absolutely right: most people do not think like I do, and therefore they do not get the results that I get. If you want to change your results, you must change your thinking. Writer William Faulkner once wrote: "Always dream and shoot higher than you know how to. Don't bother just to be better than your contemporaries or predecessors. Try to be better than yourself." I believe that most people don't miss out on life's riches because they set goals that are too high and miss them; most people have no goals at all, or they shoot too low and hit the bull's-eye of mediocrity.

My "hustle" continued throughout high school, and I eventually earned a better quality of life. I say earned because that's exactly what happened. I earned it! It was not given to me as a lot of people assumed. My work ethic allowed me to attain many different kinds of jobs, but they were all blue-collar and laborious. I did all kinds of work, and they all required being on my feet for an eight or ten hour shift, including but not limited to: flipping burgers at McDonald's, sorting packages for United Parcel Service (UPS), and washing dishes at Eastern Hills Country Club. I even worked on an assembly line making automobile air conditioner compressors. Most of these jobs were extremely difficult, but I worked with a level of anticipation and enthusiasm because I believed that someday my hard work would pay off. I believed that my efforts would help me get into college, earn a college degree, and everything in my life would change for the better. I believed that I would be able to live the American Dream. Degree Theory™ was the cornerstone of my plan and philosophy to attain the lifestyle I so yearned for. I believed that a college degree was the missing ingredient to the recipe of success, the ingredient that so many people from my neighborhood lacked. Working hard was the easy part. I didn't know of any other kind of work. I had always worked hard, so that was nothing new to me. Hard work is important, but it is not enough. You also have to work smart—a hard lesson that I learned later. I also realized that the "what" in life is more important than the "how". Once you know the "what", the "how" will reveal itself. I am living proof, because once I made a commitment to get a degree, my consciousness was alerted to many opportunities that had been right in my face the entire time.

MR. SMITH GOES TO COLLEGE

I actually earned two athletic scholarships: a junior college scholarship to play basketball for Western Texas College (WTC) in Snyder, Texas, and a two-year, full-ride to finish my undergraduate studies at City University of New York's Brooklyn College. It was a small, NCAA Division 1 basketball program located in the heart of Flatbush, Brooklyn. Many things happened over my six years of undergraduate school that made me want to drop out and go back home to Garland.

A large percentage of college students drop out and never earn their degrees. I came close to being a drop-out statistic on many occasions, but I stuck it out. The biggest issue for me was leaving my comfort zone and being on my own for the first time in my life. I had no family and no support group, but my belief in Degree Theory™ was absolute. My desire to gain a degree was stronger than my fear of loss, so I fought through the obstacles that trip up a lot of students on the quest to attain the Holy Grail: the college degree. In the spring of 1994 the day had come. My momma, my late aunt Gloria, and my cousin Ron traveled to New York to attend the commencement ceremonies on the quadrangle of Brooklyn College. I had made it—so I thought. Ironically, commencement is supposed to be the beginning of great things in your life, but for me it was the start of a downward spiral that almost took mine.

CUNY Brooklyn College Graduation 1994
My Aunt Gloria Jean, Momma, and Cousin Ronald Green A.K.A. "Pokey"

A few months after graduation and after twenty-plus months of searching for employment, I stood in a long line that wrapped around 34th Street and 7th Avenue in Manhattan with my shiny new bachelor's degree in tow. I was accompanied by five other college graduates, two of whom had Master's Degrees; we were all waiting to buy our allotment of tickets for a Depeche Mode concert at Madison Square Garden. I say allotment because we were working for a low-level mobster who ran a ring of ticket scalpers! Where did it all go wrong?

When I returned to my apartment in Brooklyn, I went up to the roof of my building and cried like a newborn. I was so afraid, hurt, and disillusioned. I was being kicked out of my housing, I had no job, I had no family and no more time to make something happen. "How can I go home like this?" I thought to myself. My momma was back home in Texas and proud as she could be. Since I was one of the only kids in my community to even go to college, there was a lot of pressure to succeed. My momma began telling tales of my success the day I drove my hooptie to West Texas to play junior college b-ball in 1988. She had spent the last six years telling everyone how well I was doing, and how successful I was. Little did she know that my life was falling apart, that I was being kicked out of my housing and had no job, or any prospects for a job! She did not know that I was actually breaking the law and violating the values and principles she taught me. I was so embarrassed and ashamed. I had let her down. I had let everyone down. I was a phony! I just couldn't believe that after all the years of sacrifice, studying, diligence, and back-breaking manual labor that there was no light at the end of the tunnel. I was actually a criminal. I thought maybe Black men were prone to criminal behavior I was from the hood—who was I trying to fool? I had become a statistic after all. My plan had failed! I was utterly and completely devastated.

My whole belief system was destroyed. How and why would God do this to me? What kind of cruel joke was this? I had wagered everything on attaining a college degree and being able to leverage it for a great job that would make all those years of work and investment worthwhile. I had no Plan B. I wasn't supposed to need one with a college degree! I heard a voice from my childhood say: "You can always fall back on your degree." How ironic, I was falling all right…right on my face. As I looked over Marine Park, Brooklyn, I thought to myself, "I'm an embarrassment to my family. I'm a failure." In that moment I felt so sick to my stomach and afraid of the future—I couldn't see a positive one for me. I thought, "What am I going to do now?" In that moment I understood how someone could take their own life. I so desperately wanted the pain to go away. I wanted the hopelessness and fear to stop torturing me. I couldn't see things getting any better. The information and plan that I had based my future on was actually incomplete. For hours I sat, cried, and contemplated my future, or lack thereof. I just could not see any light at the end of the tunnel. I though it would be so easy to just end it right here. Just jump off, and the sick feeling in my stomach, and the bleakness of my future, would go away. My aching head would stop pounding. The shame of my charade would be over. I wouldn't have to keep fighting this losing battle of life.

Part Two

Problem Identification

"Rowing harder doesn't help if the boat is headed in the wrong direction."

Kenichi Ohmae, Management Consultant

CHAPTER THREE

WHY AREN'T MORE PEOPLE SUCCESSFUL?

The previous quote by Ohmae is so appropriate for my situation and so many people in the world. I didn't lack vision, goals, discipline, hard work, persistence or any of the typical characteristics that you would think lead to success. I had all of those, and so did most of the people in East Garland who gave me the advice of "go to college." We were simply rowing the boat harder in the wrong direction.

Obviously there are lots of reasons that affect the circumstances of our lives, why things happen to people, and why people make the decisions they make, but I think there are several specific things that most people do that lead to the high levels of frustration and lack of real holistic success in the world. The most significant is just plain ignorance— specifically, the ignorance of the Natural Laws that God has put here for mankind to use. Additionally, most people are ignorant of the four levels of consciousness that we are responsible for moving through. The analogy of learning to drive is a great example of how these four levels of consciousness affect our lives.

UNCONSCIOUS INCOMPETENCE:

As children we are unconsciously incompetent concerning the operation of a car: we don't know that we don't know how to drive, nor do we care. Unconscious incompetence is a state of mind that most people today are actually stuck in. Most people don't even know that they don't know!

23

And knowing is truly half the battle. If you don't know that something is broken, can you fix it? Good sense says no, yet most people have internalized information for attaining "success" that does not lead to it, and they keep using that information. That was me for thirty years. If you keep doing what you are doing, you will keep getting what you are getting. If your beliefs and belief system are based on information that doesn't get you the results you want, then you are doomed to suffer, because you will live a life consistent with them. **YOU must evaluate your results and the information YOU used to create those results**. If the information is not working, simply make a decision to change your efforts. YOU have a choice. When YOU come into the realization that your actions are not creating the effects that YOU want, **and** when you *accept responsibility for those actions*, YOU can begin to move to the next level. I emphasized the word "you" because "you" are in control! You might not know what to do, but you should now know exactly what NOT to do. As I sat on the roof, contemplating the unthinkable, this realization hit me. I had spent the greater part of my life using a system and information that was incomplete.

Conscious Incompetence

As we grow, somewhere in adolescence we become aware of our inability to drive. We become consciously incompetent—we know that we don't know how to drive. So what did we do? We used good sense. We recognized that we were ignorant of the dynamics of driving a car and began a process to acquire the information necessary to become educated in the driving process. We developed a desire to learn how to drive, and many compelling reasons for acquiring the new skill. Even though we didn't know how to drive, our desire to drive, compelled us to move in the direction of our dominant thoughts. We took responsibility for our ignorance and chose to change it. We imagined ourselves as drivers. We set goals. We created a plan to learn the required information. We identified resources and people who could help us. We actively visualized ourselves driving. Only when you truly become sick and tired of being sick and tired with the results in your life will you move to this level.

Real holistic success in life is not possible without this level. This is where you have the epiphany or the "ah ha" moment. At this level, you become aware that you must develop a plan to gain the information you need to get what you want. You must develop plans to acquire and internalize **new** information. You must **increase** your belief systems concerning what is possible. You must short-circuit old, negative habit patterns and develop new, productive ways of thinking and being. You must identify other successful people and model their behaviors and actions. You must accept full responsibility for your life and the results you produce. You must realize, understand, and accept that every choice or non-choice that you have made, to this point, is the sole reason for your current station in life. Everything that you will have, be, or do in the future is dependent on the choices you make and the actions you take today. Once you make that commitment, you are ready to move to the next step.

CONSCIOUS COMPETENCE

You are now ready to take your driver's test and prove that you are consciously competent. This is being aware of the correct information, and also having the self-discipline and motivation to apply what you know. You make your way to the Department of Public Safety and sign up for your written driver's test and road test. All your months of preparation come down to the next ninety minutes. If you can apply what you have learned and show that you now know that you know how to drive, you will achieve your goal and earn your driver's license.

Regarding the pursuit of success in life, you will have broken the shackles of self-doubt and pity. You are free from blame and guilt. You have forgiven yourself for the mistakes and poor decisions of your past. You are now fully aware of the right information, and are willing to take responsibility to use it properly. Knowledge is **not** power! The effective application of specific knowledge is powerful! At this stage, you fully understand what to do to achieve real holistic success in life, and you do it. You take the steps necessary to plant the right seeds so that you can reap the harvest of your efforts.

UNCONSCIOUS COMPETENCE

This is the level you want to attain in every aspect of your life. This is a state of mind that produces positive results automatically. Let's examine our driving analogy one final time. Now that you have passed your tests and acquired your driver's license, you can begin a history of successful, legal driving. As the years pass and the new skills become habit, you will become unconsciously competent as a driver. Steps that you made a conscious effort to take (checking mirrors, being aware of your surroundings, firmly holding the wheel at 10 and 2, putting on your seat belt, adjusting the seat for optimal comfort, etc) will happen automatically. You will not have to think about these activities; they will become second nature. The constant repetition over time will allow you to become an expert at driving a car. I have seen people drink a cup of coffee, apply make up, change the radio, talk to someone in the back seat, and smoke a cigarette, while successfully navigating their car with their knee—not at all recommended. The point is, when you reach unconscious competence you will have developed a level of proficiency that will work automatically to get you the results you want.

The most successful people in our society have achieved this level of consciousness. Donald Trump is a great example. Donald Trump will never be financially poor, not because he is better than you or I—he just doesn't know how to be! He has learned to apply the right information regarding real estate development and leveraging other people's assets to become financially successful. He has also learned firsthand what not to do, because he lost everything and filed for bankruptcy in the late '80s. He has the good sense to use that experience to his benefit. In the late '90s he began using the same principles to expand his influence into other areas of business like television and entertainment. Donald Trump has done the right things, the right way, at the right time, repetitively for so long that financial success and high achievement have become a habit and natural product of his effort. Sowing and reaping are guaranteed by Nature and Universal Law. You can do the exact same thing. Once you make doing the right thing a habit, you will have no choice but to get the right results.

"Everybody can be great...because anybody can serve. You don't have to have a college degree to serve. You don't have to make your subject and verb agree to serve. You only need a heart full of grace. A soul generated by love."

Reverend Dr. Martin Luther King, Jr.

CHAPTER FOUR

DEGREE THEORY™

Another reason for the high levels of mediocrity is the prevalence and acceptance of Degree Theory™. The essence of the theory is that an individual with a college degree will be better prepared for life and have more opportunities than the person who does not have a college degree. This could not be further from the truth. A degree communicates many things, most notably that you can finish what you start; however, employers and the free market want people who have specialized skills and the ability to produce results. Your skill and ability to perform and produce results is what employers want, not your degree. You don't get any specialized skills as an undergraduate. You get a carbon copy, dime-a-dozen liberal arts degree that most people will never use on the job they end up working on anyway. You receive generalized information that you can obtain at you local library—for free I might add. I know that your belief system is kicking in full-time right now, but be objective for a moment and keep reading. Most people reading this book will find the following process familiar:

DEGREE THEORY™—THE SIX-STEP FORMULA FOR SUCCESS

Step 1. Get the best grades you can in high school and find a way to get to college. If you want to be successful and make the big dollars you must have a college degree. A college education will help you to become well rounded, and if you have trouble in life, you can always fall back on your college degree. No one can take your degree from you!

Step 2. Get accepted into a college or university. Use what you must to get in, including student loans, credit cards, loan sharks, federal grants, whatever... just get in! Stick it out for as long as it takes because once you have your degree, you will have the opportunity to get a job, and the world will be your oyster. And you won't get just any old job—you will get a good, well-paying job that you couldn't get without a college degree.

Step 3. Choose a position with one of the many "big companies" that will recruit you—as you will be in high demand with your degree. One of these great positions will provide you with the salary, status, and career opportunity for long-term growth and security that you always wanted.

Step 4. Work faithfully and loyally for forty to fifty years for the ethical "big company" that cares for you and it's employees. The "big company" will pay you the "big dollars" and be just as loyal to you as you are to them. Those "big dollars" will afford you the "big house", the nice cars, social status, the financially stable middle to upper-middle class quality of life you have always wanted, and most importantly, job security. They won't send your job overseas in order to get cheaper labor and make more billions for the small percentage of shareholders at the top of the food chain.

Step 5. Once you have sacrificed your whole life working for the "big company", they will reward you for your loyalty and hard work with a nice retirement party, the respect of your counterparts, a gold watch and pen set, and a "big" pension/retirement plan.

Step 6. You will live happily ever after in your "big house" with the white picket fence, your spouse, your 2.5 children, and a dog named Spot.

Does this theory sound familiar? Did this formula work for me and the other college graduates that were scalping tickets at Madison Square Garden? Did things pan out this way for the faithful employees of Enron, WorldCom, Tyco and the other greedy corporate giants? How many people do you know who are working on jobs that have nothing to do with the college degree they worked so hard and paid so much money for? Degree Theory™ is a philosophy for goal attainment that millions of people use. They are unconsciously incompetent. It is probably the most popular theory and methodology for goal attainment and success in America, if not the world. It is not until years later that most people realize that they have wasted thousands of dollars, and precious years of their lives, using **incomplete information** for goal attainment and success. Most people justify the decision to go to college with statements like: "Even though I'm not working in my field of study, I enjoyed my college experience, and it helped me to become well rounded." My response to that is: "Did you go to college to have fun and become well rounded, or did you go to improve your station in life and make money?" At that time in my life, I went for the latter, screw being well rounded! I was tired of being poor and well rounded! Besides, I don't think the majority of people go to college to become well rounded.

Let's assume that the majority of people in the US are using Degree Theory™; if so, then consider the statistics from the introduction:

If...

> *The US Department of Heath and Human Services reports that by the age of 65, for every 100 people in America, the following statistics hold true: 29 will be dead, 13 will live below the poverty level, 54 will be dependent on charity, welfare, or social security, and only 4 will be financially free.*

Then...
Degree Theory™ DOES NOT WORK!

"The definition of insanity is doing the same thing over and over, and expecting your results to change."

Albert Einstein, Scientist

When most people achieve a result that is drastically different from the one they intended, they rationalize it, justify it, or blame life for not being fair, instead of taking responsibility for making a poor decision. For years, I used a script that simply didn't work for what I was trying to achieve. I saw the result the majority of people got from following Degree Theory™, and I ignored it. Most college graduates are still paying for an education that they never really use in the occupations and jobs that they dread going to everyday, and they probably did not need the college degree to acquire the job in the first place. Go to any school in this country and ask the students what they think it takes to become successful, and the majority of them will regurgitate Degree Theory™. A college degree is a very expensive luxury, and is NOT necessary to make money, and definitely not necessary for self-actualization and personal fulfillment.

Why then? Why would parents instill Degree Theory™ when they know that life, the workplace, and our society don't work that way anymore? Remember the law of belief? You will live a life consistent with what you choose to believe, and *those beliefs form a filter for new information.* Degree Theory™ is not completely wrong; it's just incomplete. One hundred years ago and during most of the Industrial Age, it was more accurate. But now, we live in the Information Age, and that reality has changed some of the dynamics of learning, performance, child rearing, relationships, business, and everything else in our lives.

I, like most people, tried to live up to the expectations that someone else had of me; in my case it was my momma. I think my momma is like most mommas—they want to be proud of their children. They want their children to progress to higher levels of status, financial security, and success than they did. In the African-American community, education and a college degree have always been stressed because African-Americans have struggled mightily

32

for the most basic of human rights, and education was one of them. My mother grew up in a time where she was denied an education during her developmental years. My mother was eight years old when the historic *Brown vs. the Board of Education* ruling was passed, a ruling that harkened the end of federally sanctioned segregation in American schools. Even after this historic ruling, living an getting and education in rural east Texas was not easy. This reality makes Degree Theory™ even more pervasive and entrenched in the minds of the inhabitants in the African-American community.

Another major negative effect of Degree Theory™ is that it doesn't teach you to own or control anything. It teaches you to work for someone else. We are not taught to own the modes of production; we are taught to work within them, to become a cog in the machine vs. owning the machine. The problem with being a cog is that cogs are easily replaced. If it becomes cheaper to replace cogs with computers, or get cogs outside of the country, then the owners of the machine usually go the cheap route. Who cares about loyalty or what will happen to the employees who become displaced? Who cares that most of the employees have worked for thirty, forty, even fifty years making that company what it is? Who cares that those same employees helped that company make millions of dollars for the select few at the top? Sound familiar? Now, I am not condemning all big businesses as evil, but I have not worked for any of the good ones out there, so, yeah, I'm a little jaded. It also seems that a desire to reward loyalty, morality, fairness, and hard work is all but lost in business today. It seems like greed, power, and making money, regardless of the impact on the greater good, our families, communities, society, or the environment, are the objectives of many of the privileged few at the top. Degree Theory™ is a "snake oil" cure-all that does not work to create real holistic success as we have defined it, but it is so deeply ingrained in the American social psyche that people are slow to accept new information or a new philosophy. Remember, your beliefs form a filter for information that you come into contact with. Most people BELIEVE that Degree Theory™ is the key to the life they desire, therefore they filter out anything that conflicts with that belief. What are you thinking right now? What do you believe?

Am I against education? On the contrary, I am a huge advocate of education; however, education does not always encompass a college degree. Education was a major reason for writing this book. Let's be clear: I advocate understanding why we do what we do. I advocate an education in the Natural Laws of the universe that affect our world and our individual potential, laws that are balanced, neutral, and irrefutable. I advocate education that empowers and helps people to achieve their goals. I want my children and audiences to know exactly what they want to achieve, and to define what success is *before* they start taking action. Clarity of purpose is a major determinant and characteristic in high achievers. You should know exactly what you want to achieve before you start anything. Success, as we have defined it, can only be attained by doing what you love to do; that means finding your passion and manifesting your God-given potential! You must first discover your passion in life, set goals, acquire the appropriate education to achieve your goal(s), then develop the work ethic to make those goals a reality.

Examples:
- If you want to be a chef, then you need specific skills in the culinary arts.
- If you want to be an auto mechanic, then you need specific skill repairing automobiles.
- If you want to be a graphic designer, then you need specific skills in graphic design.
- If you want to be a carpenter, then you need specific skills in carpentry.
- If you want to make a ton of money, you need specific knowledge and skills in financial products, business acumen, and our economic system. (Henry Ford had minimal traditional education, but understood how to make money)

There are hundreds of examples to hammer this point home, yet we still teach Degree Theory™ to our children. You should do what successful people do: decide on your destination before you start, set clear, specific goals, get the appropriate level of education to achieve your goal(s), then take massive, all-out action to make your goals a reality. The statement "poverty is a choice" is a catalyst for debate that usually gets people to think about how they are actually responsible for, and in control of, their lives. At least they usually do once they calm down. The most common question or defense statement to poverty being a choice is: "How I am choosing to be poor, or suffer, or to have a difficult life?"

Most people say: "I work my butt off every day to support my family and do what I'm supposed to do!" Or, "Life has thrown obstacles at me that have been difficult to overcome; how is it my fault?" I know that this is a hard pill for most to swallow—I had to take that medicine myself—but it is true because human beings are "response able," or able to respond. Furthermore life and experiences in life have no meaning except the meaning you choose to give them. This could be considered the glass as half empty or half full concept. How do you see life? Do you see abundance, or do you see a lack? Whatever you decide will be true, and the choice is yours to make.

"Excellence is the result of caring more than others think is wise, risking more than others think is safe, dreaming more than others think is practical, and expecting more than others think is possible."

Anonymous

CHAPTER FIVE

LIFE IS NEUTRAL AND THE UNIVERSE IS BALANCED

The results in your life are neutral; they have no meaning. There are no good or bad outcomes, simply results. This is a concept that is even harder for people to swallow than poverty and mediocrity being a choice, but make no mistake, results have no meaning until we give them meaning, and you are "response able" for the meaning you give your results. You must develop the skill to find the opportunity in everything that happens to you. You must find, and also realize, the good in everything that happens to you. The actor Christopher Reeves became an inspiration to people around the world after he suffered an accident that left him paralyzed from the neck down. Most people would have sunk into depression, victimization, and blame. But he came out with a positive outlook. How did he do it? He redefined his existence. He gave meaning to his situation and the results of the accident. He chose to be an inspiration, instead of feeling sorry for himself. Human beings have the ability to choose how we will respond in a given situation. You and I can do the same thing, if we want to.

A few years ago, my wife and I were in a front-end collision with a young lady in Denison, Texas. As we drove eastbound on the main thoroughfare, the other driver failed to yield and pulled out in front of us at the last minute—we slammed into her at approximately 40 mph. If you have ever been in a front-end collision you know the feeling: complete disorientation for several seconds as you try to assess what has just happened. The horn was blaring as it had become stuck. There was a chemical powder everywhere from the airbags deploying, and I couldn't see very well. Once I confirmed that I was not seriously injured, I turned to my wife and checked to see if see was all right. We immediately got out of the car and checked on the driver of the other car. Everyone was alright. Then I looked at the front end of my beautiful black Mustang GT convertible. It was crumpled up like an accordion. Initially, I was absolutely furious at the young lady for pulling out in front of us like that. I actually felt my heart pumping as I was about to scream at her for putting my wife and I in danger and destroying my car, then I saw my wife and the young lady, both were physically shaking from adrenaline and the terror of being so close to severe injury or even death. We had all walked away without a scratch. I quickly put things into a different perspective. I thought: "Thank God we are all ok." Sure, my car was possibly totaled, my auto insurance premium would probably go up, and we were one hundred miles from home with no way to get back; but the information/reality I chose to focus on in that moment determined how I responded to that situation. I chose to be grateful instead of angry. You too can choose. You are "response able."

Regarding success in life, before 2001, I chose to believe and use information that was not leading me where I wanted to go. I chose to follow Degree Theory™ and use someone else's definition of success for twenty-plus years of my life, even when I was not getting the results I wanted. I chose to go to college, even when I didn't know why I was going. I chose to play basketball for Brooklyn College, even though it was not a top 50 NCAA basketball program. I chose to major in sociology, even when I didn't know how it would help me make a buck. I chose to allow fear to keep me stagnant in life, working in dead-end jobs that I hated. I chose to stay in personal relationships that were toxic because I wanted to fit in. It did not matter how hard I worked towards my goals; my plan was flawed, and I made the decision to do it all. Poverty and extended mediocrity is a choice because we can choose to do things differently. Information on personal development, wealth attainment, self-help, and success theory; biographies on the most successful people in the history of mankind; this book and many others are readily available to everyone in a free society like ours. We can choose to work on ourselves and to learn new ways of thinking. We can choose to use the Natural Laws that govern our existence. Yet, most people follow the path that was set by someone else. Most people get in the long tollbooth line of mediocrity and waste time, money, and energy following the crowd. Most people have negative attitudes about life and their future. They are unconsciously incompetent—they don't even know that they don't know! They feel like they have no control. They don't know where they are going. So the majority of people choose to use information that does not help them progress and advance in life. They choose! You chose to buy this book. You chose to read it. You must now make another choice: does this material make good sense? If so, use it! It's all about making choices. Once you validate this information as valuable, then you can use this book and the thousands of others like it that are waiting to be discovered! The choices you make, ultimately, determine the results you will get.

Defining failure is also your responsibility. You can only fail if you quit! Choose not to quit! Short-term failure is an invaluable pre-requisite for success. If you are not failing at something you are actually doing something wrong.

SMALL THINKING

Success and high achievement doesn't elude most people because they dream too big and fall short of their goals. Most people don't dream at all, or they think small. You must develop the mind-set of a high achiever, a winner, a leader, a millionaire, or a top producer well before you can ever become one. Anyone who does not embrace this "winner's mindset" will never achieve or perform at a high level. The best way to predict the future is to imagine it! Some of the greatest minds in the history of mankind were also the greatest dreamers! I've talked to thousands of people while conducting surveys and doing research for this book. The following answers are the top three responses to the question: "Where do you see yourself in the next five years?"

* "I don't know, I'm just trying to make it, man."

- * "I'm gonna do this for a while and see where it takes me."
- * "I'm just trying to get by."

I'll give you one guess as to how most of these individuals are living—they are just getting by! Most people's life story can be summed up by the following poem:

> *"I bargained with Life for a penny, and Life would pay no more, however I begged at evening when I counted my scanty store. For Life is a just employer, it gives you what you ask, but once you have set the wages, why, you must bear the task. I worked for a menial's hire, only to learn, dismayed, that any wage I had asked of Life, Life would have willingly paid."*

> Unknown poet.

Successful people don't simply desire to get by——they dream of standing on the number one spot on the podium. They visualize the winner's circle. They see themselves winning long before they win. They work consistently on themselves to make that same image a reality. You must see it, conceive it, imagine it, and visualize it well before it ever becomes a reality! All it takes is for you to see what you want (conceive), accept that it is possible for you to have (believe), and with a good plan, hard work, and determination you can get it (achieve). *"As a man thinketh in his heart, so is he"* KJV Bible. What are your dreams? Do you believe that you can have them? Do you actively imagine doing more and being more?

Right now you should be excited! You should be beside yourself with positive expectation, because NOW you know! You know several of the major keys to having it all:

- * you are response able
- * whatever the mind of man can conceive and believe it can achieve
- * you become what you think about

You have the ability to shape your life exactly the way you envision it. It starts with your mind and what you choose to believe! If you are reading this you have taken the first of many steps toward mastering yourself! If you keep doing what you're doing, you will keep getting what you're getting! It's your choice. I want you to succeed! Start working on yourself now. Visit *www. DavidLarrickSmith.com/resources* to download a free list of resources, preferred books, and audio titles that you can use to master yourself and develop a plan that will help you get what you want. You CAN Make A Difference!™ Success is waiting for you, if you choose it!

Action Exercise—Answer the following questions:

- Why do I believe what I believe about life?
- Where did my beliefs come from?
- What do I believe about myself?
- Are my beliefs empowering or defeating?

"Failure is a part of success. There is no such thing as a bed of roses all your life. But failure will never stand in the way of success if you learn from it."

Hank Aaron

CHAPTER SIX

LEARNING METHODOLOGY

As a child I remember my mother's teaching about many things. I am the man I am today because of my mother's strength, guidance, discipline, and high expectations. She talked candidly to my siblings and I about drug abuse, crime, delinquency, peer group selection, religion, civic responsibility, and behavior. In the South, this is what we call "home-training"—something contemporary parents don't seem to instill in their children anymore. One of the many colloquialisms I remember is: "A hard head makes for a soft behind!" There was no "time out" techniques employed by Ms. Alyce. She was about "whoop'in" our butts if we got out of line.

Momma would say: "Don't be hard-headed like those kids in the street, learn from their mistakes so you don't have to go through that mess!" A big part of my education, as a child, was learning through the experience of others. I learned hard lessons about life from what was going on around me. A lot of the lessons were what not to do.

Len Bias was a star basketball player for Loyola Marymount in the mid '80s. He was the first pick of the Boston Celtics in the 1986 NBA draft. Len was an icon in collegiate basketball. I imagined myself doing some of the things Len did with his life. He overcame meager standings to becoming a great professional athlete. I wanted to take care of my mother, buy her a house and retire her from her job so that she could live a life of leisure. My momma has already worked a lifetime for one little lady. She deserves the best! That was

43

a goal of mine, and for many athletes. That was, in part, the story of Len. Concerning learning methodology, trial and error is not only costly, regarding time, energy, and money—it can also be very dangerous. On draft night, Len Bias was celebrating his recent accomplishment. He was now immersed in an unfamiliar world of money, power, and influence. He had achieved one of his major goals: to change the financial destiny of his family by playing professional basketball. He was on top of the world. This should have been night of celebration, but that night, Len tried cocaine for the very first time in his life. He died later that night after having an adverse reaction to the drug.

Trial and error should not be your primary learning methodology. Some of the greatest inventions and concepts have been gleaned from trial and error, but a significant amount of studying and education also went into the process. If you want to be successful you must have a clear definition of what success is. You must become a student of success and study the habits, tactics, practices, successes, and failures of those who have gone before you. Unfortunately, trial and error is how most people choose to live and experience life. They choose to go through the pain, hurt, and disappointment themselves before a lesson is learned. As Momma would say, "The really hard-headed folks never learn". They basically do more of the things that produce the wrong results. Most people spend the majority of their time trying to figure life out, hence the horrific statistics from the US Bureau of Labor: only 4 out of every 100 people figure it out, at least financially. Well, if you are not financially free after working your whole life, and have to choose between buying medication or buying food, you probably have not achieved the other four areas that define real holistic success either.

*** SUCCESS TIP***

The most reliable path to goal achievement is to identify someone who has successfully done what you want to do, then do the things that they have done—minus the mistakes. That way you can implement all the tactics that work, and leave out all the things that do not work. Develop mentors in your areas of interest and put their experience to work for you.

ACTION ITEMS—EVALUATE YOUR PLAN

Questions to ask yourself:

- What methodology am I using? Is it working for me? Does it need revising?
- What is my plan for success and goal attainment? Is it working for me?
- Where am I going? What do I want my legacy to be? What am I contributing to the world? What am I most passionate about?
- In thirty seconds or less, list the five most important things in your life.

Each goal you set (financial, physical, emotional, spiritual, personal) will require its own plan! There will be overlap in the methods and tactics that you use to achieve your goal(s), but each goal will need a customized plan for its attainment. Visit *www.DavidLarrickSmith.com/resources* to download your FREE goal setting worksheet and action plan template.

THERE IS NO COMMON SENSE

Common sense is a curious paradox. Common sense assumes that a given result, situation, or consequence is obvious enough and simple enough that "common people" (everyone) will know about it. The result is common; therefore we all possess this trait or quality. Well guess what, I don't believe in common sense. I believe in good sense and bad sense. How many times have you heard someone say: "Well they should know not to do that, that's just common sense." Consider this: If sense were common, everyone would have some! We have a complex brain, and we make conscious decisions based on our experiences, our education, or our lack thereof. We can choose to use good sense or bad sense. Sometimes we choose no sense at all, but there is no common sense in my opinion.

EXCUSE-ITIS

Excuse-itis is the inflammation of the excuse gland, and this ailment is at epidemic proportions in this country. Something that never ceases to amaze me is when people agree with the information in this book, and then invalidate that agreement by making an excuse for their mediocre results. Most people can recite a whole list of excuses and circumstances that keep them from doing more and achieving at higher levels. Excuses are conditioned responses and will always lead to mediocrity, because excuses and blame look backward, while responsibility and accountability look forward. Most people relinquish control of their lives by not being responsible. Most people do not believe that they actually have control over their lives; if they don't have control, they shouldn't be accountable for the consequences. If you don't accept responsibility for your life, then you're playing the blame game. People vent and tell me how life and the circumstances of their lives are difficult or unfair. They blame everyone and everything but themselves for their circumstances, failures, and shortcomings. Popular phrases:

- "I don't have a degree."
- "You gotta have money, to make money."
- "It's who you know, not what you know."
- "I'm not lucky enough."
- "I need an MBA."
- "I didn't go to the right college."
- "The government should do something."

"If you want something done you'll find a way. If you don't want something done you'll find an excuse."

Donald Trump

When they're done complaining, I ask them: "who's responsible for your life?" That's when they get mad at me, but I'm ok with that. I am not trying to win a popularity contest. Reverend Dr. Martin Luther King Jr. once said: *"When making decisions, politics will ask: Is it popular? Expediency will ask: Is it safe? While conscience will ask: Is it right? As leaders we must sometimes make decisions that are neither safe nor popular, but we must make them because they are right!"*

Part Three

The Solution(s)

"The majority of men meet with failure because of their lack of persistence in creating new plans to take the place of those that fail."

Napoleon Hill, Author

CHAPTER SEVEN

RE-EDUCATION

There is nothing wrong with problem identification as long as you also offer solutions for the problems you identify. Don't complain—offer solutions! That's what this section is all about.

You are powerful, capable, and able to achieve anything that you want! The human being is the most complex creature on this planet! Human beings are literally born as geniuses, born with the most complex computer in the universe, the human brain. We are born with unlimited creativity and potential, with an advanced network of tremendous intelligence. The greatest minds in the history of mankind have only used 5 to 8 percent of their brain capacity, while the average person only uses 1 to 3 percent. Why is this? I believe it to be poor education and socialization. We have simply learned and internalized the wrong information! So, then, re-education is the key.

Where does high performance of your human machine start? In his book *Think and Grow Rich* Napoleon Hill details that human potential is unlimited if man can control his mind! Again, you will become what you think about on a constant basis. When you combine thought energy with emotion and the appropriate effort, anything is possible! The only limitations on human potential are self-imposed. This is the foundation that all personal development theory is based on, and therefore the foundation for the solutions I propose. The quality of your life will be consistent with the quality of your thoughts and your thinking! Therefore we will focus on changing your thinking.

10 Steps For Success

FORGIVE YOURSELF

In December 2001, I sat alone in my breakfast nook angry, saddened, afraid, hurt, and confused. I was so mad at myself. Outwardly I looked "successful" but inwardly, I knew that I could do more with my life. I was so disappointed that I had not achieved more with my life, or tapped into the potential that I believed was inside me. I was thirty-one years old, and I was not where I thought I should be in life. I was overweight. I had no inner peace. I was in a dead-end job, and had no career. I was not making the money I felt I deserved. I could not help my family (mother, siblings, relatives) because I was just getting by. I had tons of revolving credit card debt that I couldn't seem to get rid of. I was miserable and at the end of my rope…and it was my fault!

First, I had to forgive myself. I had to let go of the mistakes, guilt, pain, and hurt that I had shouldered for so many years. I had unwittingly used the trial and error learning method for twenty-plus years. It was time for a new primary methodology. You cannot successfully drive a car forward looking in the rearview mirror. You will eventually end up in a place you don't want to be. Your life is no different. You have to let the past go! You can't change it, but you can learn from it. The person you become tomorrow is dependent on your vision, thinking, and efforts today! I had to begin a process of re-education, and so must you. So chalk up all your past efforts, mistakes, and shortcomings as par for the course. Today you begin anew, and forgiving yourself is the first step!

ACTION EXERCISE:

#1. Take a sheet of paper and write down all the things you have been holding onto. Write down all the things that you have felt guilty, angry, cheated, or slighted about.

#2. Ball it up into a wad and throw it into the trash!

"We are what we repeatedly do. Excellence then is not an act, but a habit."

Aristotle, Philosopher

EVALUATE YOUR STATION, YOUR BELIEF SYSTEM, AND TAKE RESPONSIBILITY

I had to take stock of my situation. I had to do an assessment. I had to identify what was working and what was not. Which beliefs, activities, and support groups led to successful outcomes, and which did not. I *accepted* that my actions over the past thirty-one years had created my station and position in life, and all the things that I had done with my life—high school, the college I chose, my decisions, my efforts, my beliefs, everything that I had done to that moment—were the causes for my current situation or effects. If I did not like my situation, it was up to me to change it. I was responsible! If I wanted to change my reality and create different results over the next thirty-one years of my life, I had to change what I was currently doing, and possibly change some of what I believed in. You have to take that same medicine.

Where is your life right now? Are you happy with your station, or can you do more? Are you producing the results you want? Do your beliefs really support you, or have you bought into information that doesn't lead you where you want to go?

Questions To Ask Yourself:
* Where did my beliefs come from?
* Where am I right now?
* What do I believe about my future?
* Where do I want to be in the next: twelve, thirty-six, sixty months?

- Who's responsible for my life and happiness?

BUILDING BELIEF—WHERE DO YOUR BELIEFS COME FROM?

You were born with unlimited potential, and your parents and environment are the source of your socialization. You were not born with your current beliefs; you had to learn them through a process of repetition and socialization. Your parents, your church, your school, your friends, your environment all had a part to play in shaping your beliefs and belief system.

The Spanish philosopher Ortega stated:

> *"Human beings are the only creatures on the planet that are born into a state of disorientation with the world. All other creatures are born with instinct. Intrinsic programming that dictate and guide their behavior and development throughout their lives. They are neither aware of these instincts nor have the ability to change their behavior pursuant to them."*

When a lioness gets hungry, she goes into the jungle to stalk prey. She doesn't think: "I've had wildebeest all month, I'd rather go by the river for fish tonight." Stalking and hunting are hardwired into her make-up by instinct. Wild animals have no choice in the matter, nor are they aware or have consciousness concerning this desire to hunt; they are driven by instinct. Human beings are not. Human beings learn their behavior from their environment. We must be taught how to excel or how to fail.

This is critical, maybe the most critical information to understand. Remember, you will live a life consistent with what you believe (Law of Belief). Do you believe that you are capable of greatness? Do you believe that God has planned wondrous things for you and your life? Do you believe that you can do all things through Christ who strengthens you?

Action Exercise: Use Affirmations (verbal and written)

An affirmation is a positive personal statement that you say or write about yourself.

Example: I am a successful entrepreneur!

I am a best-selling author!

I am a winner!

I am healthy and strong!

I expect the best!

These statements have exclamation marks because you must say them out loud with conviction and power. You have learned, thought, and spoken your way into being the person you are today. You must learn, think, and speak your way to a new reality of success and prosperity in your future.

"Concerning all acts of initiative and creation, there is one elementary truth—that the moment one definitely commits oneself then providence moves too"

W.H. Murray, Explorer

DISCOVER YOUR PASSION AND SET GOALS

All personal development professionals agree, in some capacity or another, that having purpose is the key to personal fulfillment. You must take the time to find your Passion or Major Definite Purpose in life and then develop a plan to manifest that potential. In doing so, you will put yourself on a path to what psychologist Kurt Goldstein coined as self-actualization in his famous work, *The Organism*. Another famous psychologist known as the father of American humanism, Abraham Maslow, extrapolated Goldstein's work to mean the following: "The intrinsic growth of what is already in the organism, or more accurately, of what the organism is." (*Psychological Review*, 1949)

"A musician must make music, the artist must paint, a poet must write, if he is to be ultimately at peace with himself. What a man can be, he must be. This need we may call self actualisation." (*Motivation and Personality*, 1954)

Abraham Maslow is credited with developing the hierarchy of needs, described in diagram A. Maslow described four deficiency needs that all individuals must fulfill on the path to self-actualization: physiological, safety, belonging, and esteem needs. He also determined that some needs are more important than others, and depending on the circumstance in one's life, needs higher on the list will be sacrificed for the attainment of lower needs. Example: If you don't have enough food to eat, you won't worry about esteem needs and what other people think of you eating from a trash can. The challenge for individuals, then and now, is that most people never get their deficiency needs meet, and therefore never pursue higher needs like self-actualization and manifesting their potential.

Diagram A

Being Needs

Self
Actualization

Esteem Needs

Belonging Needs

Safety Needs

Physiological Needs

Deficit Needs

You must discover your Passion or Major Definite Purpose in life, and then begin the work to manifest your potential and become that person. Self-actualization can only happen when you do what you love to do most. Once you do that, you set yourself on the path to becoming the person God put you here to be. Can you see how following your passion will allow you to align your mind, your body, and your spirit? Before 2001, I had never sat down and thought about my purpose in life. I simply thought about how to make enough money so I wouldn't have to worry about it. Like most people, I was simply trying to get my basic needs taken care of.

After my epiphany that day, I began a process of soul searching to figure what I was most passionate about. The following series of questions helped me to narrow my focus and identify what was really important in my life:

- What do I like to do most?
- What gives me a sense of personal fulfillment?
- What activities give me a sense of happiness, joy, and pride?

I began to think about the activities I enjoyed most and what made me feel alive. At the time, I had so many interests that would fit the bill. I was always above average in everything that I did: basketball, carpentry, disc jockeying, cooking, sales, event management, acting and modeling, and teaching. Ask yourself the following questions:

- What do I value most in life?
- What things do I enjoy so much that I would do them for free and the satisfaction of doing them?
- What do I want my life to mean—what do I want my legacy to be?
- If I were to die in six months, how would I spend my last days?
- What statement do I embody?
- What contribution do I want to make to the world?
- Where have I had my greatest accomplishments?
- What are my greatest talents?
- What am I the best at?
- If I had 100 trillion dollars, what would I do with the influence that kind of money creates?

As I answered these questions, a common denominator appeared. A common theme of service, education, and social responsibility rang true. I care deeply about the world and the people in it. I believe that I can make a difference. I want to make the world a better place. I want to help people become better. I want to foster respect, understanding, and empathy—not just tolerance! I want to help my family, my community, and young people be the best that they can be. As I focused and concentrated on these questions…I realized my greatest successes were in public speaking and education. I love public speaking, and not because of hubris, but because it makes me feel complete. I feel like I am in my element on stage or in a classroom. It comes easily to me. It's natural for me to speak and perform. It has always been. I also have a gift for education. I have the ability to break down complex processes into smaller, more understandable steps that facilitate learning. I am a fighter, and I fight the good fight. I stand up for what I believe in. As the Godfather of soul James Brown would say: "I would rather die on my feet than live on my knees." I am an activist, an educator, and a public speaker! That is my *Major Definite Purpose*—that is why God put me here: to be a catalyst for positive change and developing his children.

I have come full circle as an activist and educator. There have been many periods in my life when the harsh realities and failures of social, community, and political activism have made me want to quit fighting for the masses. I've asked myself: *"Why fight for people who won't fight for themselves and don't believe that life can be better? Maybe I should just give in to the politics. Maybe I should sell out and forget having higher standards and principles—just get what I can get and look out for myself. Forget about the masses—let 'em suffer if they wanna suffer."* Even though I have been extremely frustrated and angry about the levels of apathy and cynicism in my environment and in this country, I keep fighting the fight. I keep going back. I continue to believe that things can be better, even when the majority of people say *nothing will change.* It's not about what other people believe; it's about what I believe. Someone else's opinion does not have to become my reality, or yours! I don't know where I will ultimately end up when the history books are written, but I do know what I want people to say: *"Dave believed, Dave cared, and Dave made a difference! He said what he meant, and meant what he said!"*

What about you? Do you know what you want history to say about you? How long will it take you to wake up and start using that information and talent that is lying dormant inside you? I believe that you already know what you need to do in order to improve your life! You know what activities you like and enjoy. You really don't need me, or anyone else, to tell you what you should do—you know! Just be honest with yourself. Most people know what they enjoy most, but they don't believe that they can be paid to do it.

Visit my website at *www.DavidLarrickSmith.com/resources* to download your "Finding Your Passion" Worksheet.

Concentrate all your thoughts upon the work at hand. The sun's rays do not burn until brought to a focus."

Alexander Graham Bell, Inventor

THE IMPORTANCE OF GOALS

What is goal setting? Goal setting is a skill, and skills can be learned. It is one of the most important skills you can develop. Unfortunately, as important as goal setting is, you will never take a class on goal setting in our public education system. All educational systems use Degree Theory™ as their primary method for achieving financial and personal success.

High achievers are systematic goal setters. Everything they do is a step towards achieving a goal. If the action, task, or choice does not lead toward their goal(s), they exercise self-discipline to delegate, screen out, or limit that activity. High achievers are often looked upon as lucky, fortunate, or as having the right pedigree, or connections; these things have absolutely nothing to do with success or goal attainment. Being successful is not about who you know or what you know, so much as, who you are and what you think!

USE YOUR GPS

GPS is an acronym for Global Positioning System. It is a military-derived technology that has found its way to civilian consumer electronics and, most notably, the automobile industry. A GPS uses geo-synchronic satellites, longitude, and latitude to triangulate the exact location of an object on the earth's surface. An array of information can be extrapolated and applied to an object that utilizes this technology including speed, distance to a destination, objects of interest along the route, and the fastest route to a destination. It is usually mounted as a display screen in the dashboard or information center of your car. It will actually talk to you in a nice voice and give you navigation information relevant to your trip as you drive. With GPS, all you have to do is put in the destination. Simply tell the GPS where you want to go, and it will audibly and visually communicate the best way to get to your destination.

It is impossible to get lost with GPS. When you go off course, the GPS computes your current position, in real time, and references the programmed destination against your current position using satellite maps of the geography; it then formulates an alternative route to get you back on track to the programmed destination in the least amount of time. It's truly amazing when you think about it. What's even more amazing is that human beings possess the exact same capability and each of us are born with it. It's your natural GPS: your ***Goal Producing System.*** You can achieve anything in life in the exact same manner that a global positioning system for your car works. The process is the same. It starts with programming your computer with a destination. Your mind is the computer, and your goals are the destinations!

PROGRAMMING YOUR NATURAL GPS—KNOW BEFORE YOU GO

People often confuse goals with objectives, milestones, or even tasks. They are not the same. Webster's dictionary defines a goal as: "the end result toward which effort is directed." Goals are tremendously important because they allow you to control change in your life. You must know the end result before you begin working. In his book *The Seven Habits of Highly Effective People*, Dr. Stephen R. Covey explains that you must begin with the end in mind, and suggests writing out your eulogy. I agree. It may sound weird, but what better way to get a clear representation of the person you want to be? When you know exactly what you want your legacy to be, you can begin doing the things that will make that description a reality.

YOUR MENTAL COMPUTER

Do you ever give any thought to how a desktop computer works? Most people don't. We just expect that the computer will work when we push the power button, and it usually does. Think of your mind as a computer. Your brain is the central processing unit (CPU), and your belief(s) and sub-conscious mind make up the disk operating system (DOS). DOS is the foundation for everything that a computer does. Without the DOS, your computer would be useless; it is the reason why your computer boots up the exact same way every time. The only way to change the boot up process is to reprogram the DOS.

The DOS on your mechanical computer came pre-programmed from the manufacturer. Your mental computer did not. Your mental DOS has been programmed by your parents, environment, and experiences through a process of socialization over several years. The functionality of your mental computer is based on this operating/belief system. Just like a mechanical computer, as long as you have a functioning DOS, your mental computer will boot up and operate the exact same way every time you turn it on/wake up. Concurrently, it is also impossible to perform any task outside the parameters that have been programmed into the DOS thus, you will live a life consistent with your operating/belief system. Therefore, if you are not realizing the results you desire in your life, you must evaluate your beliefs, or maybe even change them completely.

UNDERSTANDING YOUR MIND - THE CONSCIOUS, THE SUB-CONSCIOUS, AND THE SUPER-CONSCIOUS

The conscious mind is the critical, analytical, and thinking component of the system. It measures, calculates, discriminates, and makes decisions on what is valid or invalid. This is your input mechanism. You can take in new information when you are conscious. Whatever you say and think has an effect on your sub-conscious, because it is programmed by your thoughts and words.

The sub-conscious mind only implements what the conscious mind validates. The sub-conscious mind does not think, it does not ask questions, it simply tries to make real what the conscious mind has accepted as valid. Regardless of the accuracy of the information taken in by the conscious mind, the sub-conscious mind tries to bring it into reality. You must be extremely careful of what you say about yourself and what you allow yourself to be exposed to on a constant basis because you are programming your mental computer for problems or possibilities.

The super-conscious mind is like plugging your computer into a super-high-speed internet connection. The super-conscious has been called many things, including flow, being in the zone, and the infinite intelligence. This is where you can tap into vast amounts of information, energy, and creativity. Some of the greatest minds in the history of mankind have credited the super-conscious for their accomplishments and discoveries.

Control, Alt, Delete—*Refer to the answers you uncovered in Step Two.*
You change your beliefs and reprogram your sub-conscious mind by using verbal and written affirmations in your conscious state. What you choose to accept as real and true in your conscious mind is relayed to your sub-conscious mind as fact, and the sub-conscious works to bring that image into reality; therefore to control your reality and become the new person you want to be, you must see, think, imagine, write, and speak it into reality! Success

doesn't start with money, it doesn't start with a degree, it doesn't start with the people you know. It starts with what you consistently focus on. Money, education, and connections are all tools in your toolbox that will be used along the way, but your ability to succeed does not start with them, nor is it completely contingent upon them; ever heard the saying: "where there's a will, there's a way"?

Success Tips:

- Never say anything about yourself that you do not want to be true
- Set goals. Know exactly what you want to achieve, have, or become before you start.
- Believe! Develop 100 percent confidence that you can achieve your goal(s).
- Put in the right effort. Use the right information and tools at the right time.
- Evaluate your results. Do your efforts take you closer to your goal, or move you farther from it?
- Never quit. Understand that short-term failure is part of the success process.

The subconscious mind is programmable through your conscious mind using the following tactics:

- verbal and written affirmation
- visualization
- auto-suggestion

Visit my website, *www.DavidLarrickSmith.com/resources,* to download your FREE Smith Development Systems "Goal Setting" Worksheet.

"If one advances confidently in the direction of his dreams, and endeavors to live the life that which he has imagined, he will meet with a success unexpected in common hours."

Henry David Thoreau

ELIMINATE F.E.A.R. AND TAKE CONTROL OF CHANGE

Two major motivators for human behavior are the fear of loss and the desire for gain. Human beings naturally seek comfort; therefore, we don't gravitate towards activities that make us uncomfortable. You must understand that being comfortable being uncomfortable is an indispensable characteristic of high achievers. All of the fears that disrupt your success and keep you stuck in life are self-imposed limitations. However, the Law of Belief makes these limitations real. The next time you feel the emotion of fear, consider this: the acronym F.E.A.R. stands for False Evidence Appearing Real.

Fear keeps most people immobilized in mediocrity. High achievers and winners constantly push the envelope to be, have, and do more! They are common people with uncommon desire for gain, a vision of greatness, and a belief in themselves. They take calculated risks. They innovate and defy convention.

Where is the fruit on a tree? Is it close to the strong and sturdy trunk, or out on the less sturdy (often times flimsy) limb of the tree? Winners are not fearless; they just don't allow fear to stop them from taking action. They develop the courage to feel the fear and take action regardless. You eliminate fear by taking action.

CONTROLLING CHANGE

Two of the biggest fears human beings confess to having are the fear of public speaking and the fear of change. People fear change because they think and feel that life will be worse after a change, which compels them to stay in their comfort zone. Thus, their fear of loss is stronger than their desire for gain. Remember, goals allow you to control the direction of your life and the direction of the change. Without goals you're like a ship with no rudder. Without a rudder (goals) you will float aimlessly, wandering in any direction, as the winds and tides of life push you around. Sometimes you will find calm waters and other times, hostile territory, but the whole time you will have absolutely no control over where you go because you have no rudder! Goals provide you with the direction and the destination you need to eliminate the anxiety of not knowing how you will end up. It's the not knowing that scares people. Do you have clear, concise goals? If you don't, then you are wandering. You are relinquishing control of your life to chance. How risky is that? Always begin with the end in mind. Set goals before you start. If you don't know where you are going, stop moving, do an assessment, decide on a course, then begin your journey again. Happy sailing!

"We are what we think. All that we are arises with our thoughts. With our thoughts we make our world."

The Buddha

STEP FIVE

CONTROL YOUR ATTITUDE

Attitude is defined as "the position or bearing as indicating action, feeling, or mood." Our actions, feelings, or mood also determine the actions, feelings, or mood of those around us. Your attitude communicates to the environment what you expect from other people and the world. You will get back from the world exactly what you put into the world (Law of Return). If you are smiling and cheerful and have an attitude of positive expectation (Law of Expectation), your mannerisms will communicate positively to the world around you, and people will respond to you positively. Conversely, if your attitude is sour and you suffer from stinking thinking and expect negative outcomes, your physical mannerisms and non-verbal communication will reflect your negative expectations, and people will respond to you according to your negative outward expression. Additionally, you will not see any of the opportunities for excellence that are happening around you.

Our surroundings will always reflect our attitudes and expectations. So it's fair to say that our attitudes are derived from our expectations about results, that our feelings regarding the outcome of any given situation will determine our attitude. The better we feel about the outcomes, the better our attitude will be. The majority of people in society are ignorant of this principle, or they choose to filter it out because it conflicts with what they have chosen to believe. Most people don't believe that they have control over their lives, let alone their attitudes. They don't give meaning to what happens to them. Most people simply react based on a conditioned response to stimuli or an event.

Have you ever approached a tollbooth and noticed a long line of cars backed up at the booth, while right next to the long line of cars, there is another, completely empty tollbooth available? We habitually go with the flow. Sociologists call this contagion of a crowd. This is a critical distinction between high performers/winners and low performers/whiners. Leader's don't go where the path takes them: leaders go where there is no path, they set goals, then blaze a trail!

The key to controlling your life is controlling your thoughts and controlling what your conscious mind dwells upon. You can't always control what pops into your mind, but you can control what you dwell upon. This principle is what makes goals and goal setting so important. When you have goals, your life has direction. You know exactly where you want to end up. If you can concentrate on the good things in your life and where you are going, versus feeling frustrated, angry, and sorry about where you currently are, then your attitude will be positive. Thus, positive goal setting allows you to control change because you can map out where you want to go in reference to where you are. You can then develop the resources, education, money, and people you need to get what you want. Having a clear destination and keeping your thoughts focused on that destination is a major step.

Ultimately, life is not about what happens to you, but how you respond to what happens to you! Attitudes are habitual behavior. We develop them through our environment and from our experiences. You can decide right now if you are going to control you attitude, by controlling what you think about on a consistent basis, and by controlling what you expect from yourself and from life. Do you expect to succeed? Do you expect the best? Do you see yourself winning? Can you envision enjoying the finer things in life and helping your family and friends to do the same? Can you imagine being stress-free and having all the things you have ever wanted? If you can, then you can have it! It all starts with what you think and believe is possible for your life. By knowing your purpose in life and diligently working toward the attainment and manifestation of it, you will be able to control the direction of your life.

You can have a clear, positive outlook and positive expectations, because you know exactly where you are going and what you will eventually achieve! You can be excited about your future, because you have seen it! None of this will happen overnight. This is a process of nature—sowing and reaping. You must begin sowing the right seeds consistently, and you must be diligent. Carefully tend to your crop through the season, and you will have a harvest of success-GUARANTEED! "The best way to predict the future is to imagine it!" Unknown poet.

"It is not the strongest of the species that survive, nor the most intelligent, but the one most responsive to change."

Charles Darwin, Biologist

BUILD DESIRE AND UNDERSTAND MOTIVATION VS. INSPIRATION

Now, the answers and steps to becoming successful are actually very simple. The application of this information is what trips up most people. Over time you have learned and developed many habits. Some good, some bad, and now I'm telling you to just change them. People say to me, "Dave, you make it sound so easy, you don't understand, it's not as easy as you make it sound". Consider this: change can be easy, or difficult; it's simply a matter of your perspective. Accepting and making a change is simply a matter of having enough compelling reasons to do so.

Example:

Under average circumstances, most of us would not eat discarded day-old food out of a trash can. However, what if you fell upon hard times and had not eaten anything in three weeks? How would you respond then? How quickly would you change your position on eating from the trash? Would it be easy or hard to do? It's all about perspective. My question to you is: "How hungry are you for success?" Desire is the starting point for real change. When desire is compelling enough, ordinary people will do extraordinary things. Are you really sick and tired...of being sick and tired? What are your reasons for changing your life? What are your motivations?

WHERE DOES MOTIVATION COME FROM?

Motivation is intrinsic. It is an internal stimulus. Inspiration is extrinsic. It comes from your environment. You have your own motivations—your own reason for doing everything that you do. I am not a motivational speaker, and this is not a motivational book. My intent as an author is to INSPIRE you! I want to remind you of your internal motivations (your reasons) to take action. Human beings take action for many reasons: family, parents, fear, significant others, community, money, status, material items…the list goes on. I am making an assumption that the definition of real holistic success that I detailed in the introduction is something that you want to achieve. I believe that real holistic success is one of your motivations, so I'm speaking to that right now. The point here is having compelling reasons to take action will make doing so that much "easier." My hope is that reading this book and my story will inspire you. If you don't have enough compelling reasons for making a change in your own life, or for doing what you know needs to be done, then it will be very hard for you to make any type of change. A wise man once said: "You can lead a horse to water, but you can't make him drink." Are you thirsty?

Action Exercise: Make a list of all the reasons for changing your life.
- Why do you need to achieve your goals?
- How will your life be different when you achieve your goals?
- Who will benefit from it?
- What will happen if you don't make a change?

"Some men see things as they are, and say, why? I dream of things that never were, and say, why not?

George Bernard Shaw, Author

STEP SEVEN

DEVELOP A PLAN

By now you know that I have a saying or quote for just about everything. Here's one to exemplify the importance of planning: "If you fail to plan, you are planning to fail!" Anonymous.

Think about all the planning that went into your last vacation. The average person spends many months planning a vacation, and normally, they have a very clear idea and mental representation of what being on vacation will be like. The vacation starts out as a wonderful visual image of you participating in your favorite leisure activity. You imagine yourself relaxing on a beach or near a pool. You have the standard tropical fruity drink with the umbrella garnish. The air is light and clean, with a slight scent of coconut suntan lotion and sea spray. You don't really know what time it is, and you don't care, because you don't have to be anywhere! Your only concern is: "Should I have the grilled sea bass or the fish tacos with mango salsa for lunch?" That image, the desire for that vacation experience, will propel you to take action. Now that you know what you want to experience, you need to get your ducks in a row to make it happen. You will make a list of all the things that need to happen in order to get to the beach and the fruity drink: how much will it cost, where are the best places to visit, how will you get there, will you take the kids, what hotel will you stay in, should you buy an online package or do it all yourself—and this list goes on. Once you have your list, you must prioritize it. What needs to happen first and when? You will assign responsibilities to your spouse/ significant other and travel agent. You will set up timelines and due dates. You will also develop a mechanism to measure the progress of each action item on your list and those that you have delegated. You NOW have: a goal, a set of objectives, and a list of tasks. All these components together combine to make a plan that will make your vacation a reality and a success.

Once all this is in place you will find yourself frequently using the images of your soon-to-be-vacation as motivation, and a reminder of what's to come. You might daydream and visualize yourself drinking rum punch and dancing badly to calypso music on the Yellowbird Boat Rum Punch Cruise. When circumstances in your life become overbearing you will remember your plans and think to yourself "I'm going on vacation in a few months." When your boss and job get on your nerves, you will use the image of sandy beaches, palm trees, and parasailing as your escape from reality. You will repeat this mental exercise whenever life gets frustrating or overwhelming; your thoughts of vacation will soothe and calm you. You will frequently review your list of objectives with your fellow vacationers to discuss the progress of each assigned task. You will assess efforts, quantify results, and make modifications to the plan when things get bogged down. All of this will happen to ensure that come your vacation date, everything goes off without a hitch and that you have two fruity drinks with pineapple garnish waiting for you! Yes, I like fruity drinks, if you did not guess by now. A sad reality is that the average person spends more time, energy, and effort planning one or two weeks of vacation than they spend planning and mapping out their lives!

You should also realize that my advice and these suggestions are not difficult to understand; this is not rocket science! If you drive this far on your journey to success, and have no plan, you will undoubtedly take a detour. Think of your plan as your road map for success. Your goals are the destinations, your desire is the fuel for the trip, and your motivation is your sustenance for the long haul.

"I cannot teach anybody anything; I can only make them think."

Socrates

STEP EIGHT

BELIEVE THE PLAN AND GET COMMITTED

Remember the Law of Belief? A lack of belief inevitably leads to a lack of commitment. Today, people get commitment confused with making a contribution. The difference can be exemplified by examining a typical breakfast. A chicken only makes a contribution when creating breakfast, but if you have bacon, a pig has to make a commitment! There is a huge difference.

Concerning high achievement and success, when you leave room for plan B—you are telling yourself and your sub-conscious mind: "I don't believe that plan A will work, so I better have a back-up plan". This is folly! You cannot have it both ways. Either you believe that you can achieve what you set out to do, or you don't! We confuse nature and the universe by asking for something with our mouths but not really believing in our hearts and minds that we can get it. It's called false hope. When you have belief and faith, you don't need hope because you know that you will get what you ask for. Philippians 4:13 states: "I can do all things through Christ who strengthens me." I get into trouble with my fellow Christians because I take them to task about this scripture and their performance. They profess to believe, yet when we discuss success and winning in life, many of them blame others, circumstance, pedigree, the devil, and everything else for their limited station in life or their lack of success and happiness. They have a lack of belief in themselves, and that lack of belief short-circuits their success. They argue with me about all the reasons, obstacles, and inequity in the world. At that point, I remind them of Philippians 4:13. It is not my intention to be argumentative;

however, the truth is incontrovertible: if you argue for your limitations, you get to keep them.

Take marriage for instance, mine particularly. I have committed 100 percent to my wife and to our marriage. Marriage is not so much about feelings, because feelings change. Marriage is about commitment. I understand my marriage to be a covenant with God. I have no plan B for my marriage. I do not have a back-up girlfriend. I do not have a relationship with an old flame from college that I maintain in the event that my marriage doesn't work out! I have committed 100 percent to making my marriage work. I made a 100 percent commitment to making it what I want it to be. There is no compromise on what my relationship with my wife will be. I know exactly what I want it to be. I believe that I know exactly what she wants it to be. We invest daily in our lives together: emotionally, physically, and spiritually. I use the word invest, not sacrifice, intentionally. When you invest you create a return—you sow a seed. There are no returns on a sacrifice. A sacrifice is simply a trade: this for that. We invest in each other, and therefore we reap the harvest of a healthy, fulfilling, progressive relationship and marriage. We are not reactive to life and our lives together. We actively visualize, communicate, and listen to each other's needs; we then work to anticipate those needs. Is our marriage perfect? No, not at all, but do I think we have created an environment for our relationship to thrive, grow, and evolve as we do? You bet I do! You must do the same with each goal you set and strive for in your life.

Plan B is a fallacy perpetuated by those with limited thinking and weak beliefs! None of the great inventions or accomplishments in the history of mankind were achieved by limited thinking or limited beliefs. In order to win and be a winner, you must believe in yourself—PERIOD! Right now you have to analyze what you have chosen to believe. Do you believe in yourself? Do you think big? Are you a winner? Do you work as smart as you do hard? Do you work on your personal development every day? Or are you: going through the motions, hoping that your luck will change, hoping to make the right connections, hoping for someone in your support group to make it, so they can then "hook you up"? Are you hoping, or do you believe? You must make the commitment to identifying your passion and manifesting your potential! The following quote by Himalayan explorer W. H. Murray exemplifies the power of commitment:

> *Until one is committed, there is hesitancy, the chance to draw back, always ineffectiveness. Concerning all acts of initiative (and creation), there is one elementary truth, the ignorance of which kills countless ideas and splendid plans: that the moment one definitely commits oneself, then providence moves too. A whole stream of events issues from the decisions, raising in one's favor all manner of unforeseen incidents, meetings and material assistance, which no man could have dreamt would have come his way.*

The average person is not committed to anything. The average person does not spend enough time, if any, developing themselves and their minds. Today, we live in a world that blindly accepts what our circumstances, environment, and media tell us. The majority of people are complacent and afraid. We allow the opinions of other people to become our reality. I say to you: if Gandhi can change the face of India and British rule, then YOU can achieve your goals. If the Reverend Dr. Martin Luther King Jr. can change the face of race relations in the United States, then YOU can win in life! This list could go on for days; the point is, they were ordinary human beings just like you and me. They had compelling reasons to take action. These men decided that they would do whatever it took to make a difference. They knew what they would live and die for. They believed in themselves, worked on themselves, set goals, and worked toward their goals relentlessly. They understood the results they got from their efforts and made adjustments when needed. They developed self-discipline to do the important things first and consistently. They were COMMITTED! They had FAITH! They BELIEVED in themselves! They were just like you and me: ordinary people, who did extraordinary things. The multi-billion dollar question is: Do you believe that you can do the same?

"If you are going to achieve excellence in big things, you develop the habit in little matters. Excellence is not an exception, it is a prevailing attitude."

Colin Powell, Statesman

STEP NINE

EXECUTE THE PLAN

This step will be one of the most challenging for you because now you have to put your money where your mouth is. As we say in the south: "Gir'r Done!" You have to DO IT! I discovered my passion in 2001, and it took me six years to shake off the twenty-five-year-old negative habits that were limiting my potential. I chose to struggle for an additional six years. I chose! I chose to complain. I chose to feel entitled to all the pain, discomfort, stress, disfunctionality, and lack of success I had experienced for so long. I chose it by holding on to it. All I had to do was forgive myself and let it go. I can't change the past, and neither can you. Once I let the pain go, I was able to raise the anchor, chart a course, and begin sailing toward my inner greatness! The journey of a thousand miles begins with the first step. Remember your list of reasons why you need to get this done. Remember the Law of Attraction and that you will get what you think about most. Remember that you are God's child and you were born to do great things! Just as God spoke the earth into existing with the power of his voice, as a child of God you have that exact same power to create an existence just as you envision and speak it.

Use the following declaration as part of your daily oath, prayer, meditation material, or verbal affirmation. You must say this like you mean it: with feeling, conviction, and power. Start right here, right now, right where you are—make the following commitment to yourself:

> *I commit myself to the achievement of my goals and the manifestation of my potential! I will pursue my goals with passion, self-discipline, enthusiasm, and urgency for the betterment of myself, my kindred, my community, my nation, and my planet. I am capable, and I am empowered to achieve anything that my mind can conceive and believe. I choose to believe! This creed I swear to uphold until my potential is realized, and my goals are achieved, so help me God!*

Visit *www.DavidLarrickSmith.com/resources* to download your FREE frameable copy of this success declaration.

You have come a long way. You need to keep in mind that the process of attaining real holistic success is not a destination, it's a journey. You did not become the person you are today overnight, and you will not become the winner you want to be overnight either. There is no quick fix. A lot of people today want credit for participation, but in the classroom of life you only get credit for completing the lessons. Remember in grade school, how your overall grade was made up of several areas: daily participation, quizzes, behavior, and the final exam? Well guess what, this is the final exam! If you fail to execute, it's not the end of the world, but you might have to repeat the class! Remember, it took me six years to get it together even when I knew what to do. I wrote this book so you don't have to waste any more time.

"We first make our habits, and then our habits make us."

John Dryden, Poet

STEP TEN

DEVELOP THE WINNING EDGE

The majority of the work I propose requires mental effort. There is minimal physical effort needed. You must develop self-discipline to consistently do the right things on purpose all the time. Rich or poor, smart or not so smart, black or white—Universal Law affect us all the same way. By using this information you can create your own good luck. Luck is merely the intersection of preparedness and opportunity. Since there is no lack of opportunity in the world the question becomes: are you prepared? You will be if you develop the winning edge.

The Winning Edge Concept states that small changes in your effort can equate to huge difference in your results. To begin manifesting your potential, huge changes in your life are not required, nor are they practical. You need to use the law of accumulation and the conservation of momentum to get things rolling. The Winning Edge Concept is the key.

Example:
I live in the suburbs east of Dallas, and I have clients in downtown. If I leave my house five minutes after 7:00 a.m., my commute will be approximately sixty to seventy-five minutes. However, if I leave just five minutes before 7:00 a.m., the same commute takes approximately twenty-five to thirty minutes. A very small change in my effort equates to a significant difference in my commute. A horse race illustrates this point even better. Let's say that the race is so close that a photo finish is required. The first place finisher's prize purse

99

will be exponentially greater than the rest of the field. The question to ask yourself is: was the first place finisher's performance exponentially better than the second or third place finishers? The answer is no. The winner was merely a little bit better than the competition. It was being a little bit better, doing a little more during the race, essentially making small adjustments in effort, that made the huge difference in the results. That is what you must now do! You must develop the winning edge. You now have the information. You now have the formula and the steps. You must start making the small changes today that will equal huge differences for you tomorrow.

You now have a tool, but this tool is worthless unless you put in the effort and use it properly. Are you working on the project of your life with a hammer when you really need a screwdriver? WOW...you should be EXCITED—I am! I can hardly finish typing. If you have followed the steps, you should be able to see and envision a better life for yourself. If you can see it, you can be it! You can create a life just as you imagine it right now! It starts with what you think and believe. That's it. Start right where you are.

Are you willing to pay the price? Are you willing to accept the calculated risk and take the leap? There is no line of credit for success; the cost must be paid in advance. Everyone who is serious about creating real holistic success must pay the piper first. No exceptions!

> *"Ask, and it will be given you; search, and you will find; knock, and the door will be opened for you."*
>
> Matthew 7:7

My fellow readers, make no mistake, this is a Divine work. I believe that God has tasked me to teach and share this message, but you have to be open to hearing it. For many years, my ignorance and arrogance kept me from seeing and hearing the messages from God that were all around me. He did not talk to me directly. I didn't hear a voice from the clouds that said "Write a book for my people!" But when you know, deep down in your being...you know! God has given us cognitive reasoning and the ability to choose. We can choose to use the wealth of information that is available to us all, or we can ignore it—it's all about choice. I can only hope that this work spoke to you. I can only hope that it provided you with the needed INSPIRATION to help you take action! CHOOSE to believe, CHOOSE to win. Remember…You CAN Make A Difference!™

ABOUT THE AUTHOR

David Larrick Smith is a simple man, who says what he means, and means what he says! David is a premier inspirational speaker and personal development professional. Known for his success as a entrepreneur and community advocate, David brings real world solutions, tangible tactics, and old-fashioned "good sense" to every program he produces. Drawing on 15 years of experience as a top salesman, marketing executive, and business development consultant, David delivers compelling thought-provoking presentations that have inspired thousands. He is owner of David Larrick Smith Enterprises and the founder of the SMITH Foundation for Excellence, an organization dedicated to helping people manifest their GOD-given potential.

Praise for David and Straighten Up and Fly Right

"David has done an amazing job transferring his passion for sharing timeless tips, techniques, and methodologies for living a more successful life. From the spoken word that I have heard him deliver, to the written word in Straighten Up and Fly Right. This book is a must read for those searching for the path to success as well as for those of us who recognize that we need to continue reading and taking advantage of opportunities that will support us in keeping ourselves inspired so that we can continue to grow and evolve."

Ms. Betty Artis, Marketing Manager
Fair Park / Dallas Parks and Recreation Department

"You have made a difference! Not only in my life, but in so many others. Outstanding! Hundreds of students have realized that they can make the world a better place."

Mrs. Judy Garrett, School Teacher
South Garland High School, Garland Independent School District

"David was inspirational and invigorating, he gave my team and I a new sense of empowerment with his thought provoking presentation. His ability to find the greatness in all my staff and myself will keep inspiring me to never accept things at face value, but to look deeper inside people for their fullest potential."

Mr. Jonathan E. Forgione
Financial Center Manager, Washington Mutual